i

Whom the Son Sets Free:

Basics of Deliverance and Emotional Healing

By

Dr. Damian A. Hinton, Sr., MDiv, MTh, DMin

Published by: Kingdom Scribe Editors
ISBN: 9798267031899
Cover and Interior Design: Kingdom Scribe Editors
Printed in the United States of America

i

Acknowledgments

I want to thank the Lord Jesus Christ for His matchless power to save, heal, and deliver. To my wife, Overseer Cheryl Hinton, your unwavering support and spiritual strength are a constant reminder of God's grace in my life. To the pastors, elders, ministers, and saints of Life Changing Ministries and the Apostolic Network of International Churches and Ministries—thank you for your faith, intercession, and commitment to freedom. Special thanks to every deliverance minister, scholar, and teacher who has paved the way and shared their wisdom. To those who shared their stories and experiences—your courage brings light to others still fighting in darkness.

Table of Contents

FORWARD

I am so very honored to do the forward on this book, *Whom the Son Sets Free: Basics of Deliverance and Emotional Healing.* As you read this book, you will understand more about the subject of deliverance. Deliverance is a subject that many people shy away from because of fear. However, after reading this book by Dr. Damian Hinton, whom I have known for over 15 years, you will be able to approach deliverance with a sense of understanding that you can do this yourself. It will give you the boldness to confront the things of the enemy.

This book is not only for individual study but can also be used for small groups and as a teaching tool. It is suitable for those beginning their walk with understanding the subject of deliverance, as well as for those who are intermediate and advanced. The scriptures used throughout the book are truly on point and provide a solid foundation for understanding and applying the principles of deliverance.

I have known Dr. Damian Hinton for over 15 years and have watched him perform numerous deliverances. I will share one quick story with you. There was a time when someone I knew was overshadowed by the enemy and a demonic force. Dr. Damian Hinton did not even know what was going on, as he was in another room. When he came into the room, he immediately went over and hugged them so tightly with love that the demon was instantaneously eradicated from that person. As the tears fell from that individual, the demonic entity was never seen again. That person was a close family member of mine. From that moment forward, I understood and grew even more in my knowledge under Dr. Hinton's guidance. I then understood that you could force darkness out with pure love.

As you read this book, I advise you to take a highlighter and a pen and paper because you will want to take notes and highlight key passages and instructions. One of my favorite things about this book is the declarations that follow each chapter. I warn you that as you read and come to the declarations, you will be compelled to recite them over yourself. You may be surprised to find that some things you read about may be dwelling within yourself or overshadowing you.

Once again, it is such a great honor to endorse this book. I highly recommend this book for its insightful content and its ability to bring light to dark situations. Enjoy this impactful read!

By Apostle Samonia Whisonant
Mountain Be Removed Outreach Center
Harrisburg PA

PREFACE

One of the greatest challenges for any spiritual leader is watching men and women—especially young men and women—struggle with deep spiritual wounds. These wounds are often not of their own making. Some are inherited through generational iniquity and family transgression. Others are the product of trauma experienced in the womb, shaped by environments of violence, neglect, and rejection. Still others emerge through societal oppression, ungodly soul ties, abuse, or direct involvement in practices that unknowingly opened doors to the demonic.

Over the years, I have grieved as I witnessed gifted, intelligent, and called individuals wrestle with invisible chains—tormented in thought, plagued by fear, bound in addiction, or paralyzed by cycles of shame. These are not strangers to the faith; many are Christians—saved, Spirit-filled, and sincere—yet still in bondage. This reality compelled me to write this book.

Whom the Son Sets Free: Basics of Deliverance and Emotional Healing is more than a theological treatment of spiritual warfare. It is a pastoral call to confront bondage with biblical truth, spiritual authority, and Christ-like compassion. It is my conviction that deliverance is not a fringe ministry, but a central part of Jesus' earthly mission—and it remains essential for the Church today.

This book is written to equip pastors, leaders, counselors, intercessors, and believers with a foundational understanding of the unseen war that wages in human lives. It offers biblical insights, historical perspectives, and practical strategies to engage in the ministry of healing and freedom. You will find real-life stories, Scripture-based principles, application moments, and tools for discernment and sustained victory.

Deliverance is not about theatrics or fear—it is about restoring men and women to their rightful identity in Christ. It is about seeing the bound set free, the broken made whole, and the wounded restored to purpose. It is about closing the doors that the enemy has exploited and building a life of ongoing spiritual health and authority.

May this book awaken your awareness, sharpen your

discernment, and inspire you to step into the liberating power of Jesus Christ. May you become not only a recipient of freedom, but also an agent of it. And may your life—and those you lead—reflect the fullness of this truth: *"Whom the Son sets free is free indeed."*

Until we see Him face to face,

Dr. Damian A. Hinton, Sr., MDiv, MTh, DMin

INTRODUCTION

Called to Be Free

> "It is for freedom that Christ has set us free..." — Galatians 5:1

Many believers today walk in the power of salvation but not the fullness of freedom. Jesus came not only to save souls but to liberate lives from bondage—emotional, spiritual, and demonic. Whom the Son Sets Free is a practical guide rooted in Scripture that reveals how believers can understand and engage in the ministry of deliverance. Drawing from the ministry of Jesus, the early church, and insights from church fathers, this book equips readers to identify demonic activity, break free from spiritual oppression, and walk boldly in the liberty of Christ.

God's heart for liberty is profoundly revealed in passages like Isaiah 61:1 and Luke 4:18. These scriptures speak of "liberty to the captives," highlighting a divine intention for the complete release and restoration of His people. The Hebrew word for liberty,

Deror or daror, carries a rich meaning: it signifies a state where one is free to flow, sparkle or radiate with the Glory of the Lord (Isaiah 9:2). This deep understanding of liberty connects God's intention to our human experience, moving beyond mere physical release to a vibrant spiritual flourishing.

The purpose of deliverance and healing, as explored in this book, is far more comprehensive than simply 'casting out demons.' It encompasses a holistic restoration of the individual – distinguishing between physical, emotional, and spiritual freedom. This ministry aims to bring believers into the full, abundant life that Christ promised.

However, the topic of deliverance is often shrouded in myths and fears. Many misconceptions exist, ranging from sensationalized portrayals to fear-mongering and the notion of 'a demon behind every bush.' This book seeks to dispel these myths, emphasizing instead God's boundless love, unwavering power, and divine protection over His children. We must understand that freedom isn't just for the lost; it's for the saints too. While salvation justifies us, there is an ongoing process of sanctification and a continuous need for spiritual cleansing in the believer's life. This book will illuminate the path from initial salvation to practical, lived-out freedom in every area.

Looking Ahead

Understanding this foundation—that God's design is for radiant, full-spectrum freedom—sets the stage for receiving and ministering deliverance with wisdom, confidence, and compassion. As we now turn to Chapter 1: The Freedom God Designed, we will delve deeper into this divine blueprint for liberty.

Chapter 1

THE FREEDOM GOD DESIGNED

The concept of freedom is woven into the heart of God's plan for humanity. From the earliest pages of Scripture to the triumphant declarations of the New Testament, liberty is portrayed not merely as release from bondage but as restoration to divine purpose. To fully embrace the freedom God designed, we must begin by understanding its biblical foundation and spiritual significance.

A Deeper Look at Deror

At the core of this biblical vision of freedom is the Hebrew word Deror דְּרוֹר (or daror), used in key passages such as Isaiah 61:1 and Leviticus 25:10, particularly in relation to the Year of Jubilee.[1] This word

---

[1] Deror (Hebrew: דְּרוֹר) is a Hebrew term meaning "liberty" or "freedom," particularly used in reference to divine release from bondage, debt, or captivity. It appears most notably in Leviticus 25:10 in connection with the Year of Jubilee: "And you shall consecrate the fiftieth year, and proclaim liberty [deror] throughout the land to all its inhabitants..." The

conveys more than release from physical captivity—it implies a return to original design and dignity. Deror describes a person not merely unchained, but radiant— free to flow, sparkle, and shine with the glory of the Lord, just as light shined into darkness (Isaiah 9:2). This radiant freedom is not just about escape from sin—it's about becoming who God made us to be.

In Leviticus 25:10, the call to proclaim liberty throughout the land was a divine declaration that every 50th year would restore people, property, and purpose. This Old Testament pattern finds its ultimate fulfillment in Jesus Christ, who announced in Luke 4:18 that He came to "proclaim liberty to the captives." He came not only to remove what binds us, but to restore what was lost.

---

word carries connotations of not only emancipation but also restoration of identity, inheritance, and social position. Linguistically, deror is derived from a root that implies "flowing freely" or "running swiftly," symbolizing the removal of restriction and the release of blessing. Theologically, it reflects God's character as Redeemer and Deliverer who initiates holistic freedom. Brown, Francis, S. R. Driver, and Charles A. Briggs. A Hebrew and English Lexicon of the Old Testament, s.v. "דְּרוֹר (deror)." Oxford: Clarendon Press, 1906. See also Strong's Concordance, H1865.

From Captivity to Glory

Biblical freedom is not a one-time event—it is a journey. It begins with salvation but continues through sanctification, leading us deeper into alignment with God's will. The journey from captivity to glory is marked by a transformation: from hiding in the shadows of bondage to walking boldly in the light of God's presence.

True freedom, then, is not merely defined by what we are liberated from, but by what we are called into. It is the vibrant reality of living with purpose—a purpose anchored in God's original intent for humanity. This freedom invites us to step fully into our identity as image-bearers of God (imago dei), crafted to mirror His character, creativity, and love in the world.

To be free is to participate in the ongoing story of redemption, unshackled from the burdens of shame and fear, and equipped to pursue the good works God has prepared for us. It means that our lives are no longer dictated by the wounds or limitations of the past, but are instead animated by the Spirit, who empowers us to walk in righteousness, peace, and joy.

This kind of freedom is dynamic and transformative. It enables us to reflect the light of God's presence in our daily choices, relationships, and vocations. Rather than drifting aimlessly or living in reaction to circumstances, we become agents of His Kingdom—people who embody hope, justice, and compassion. In living out this freedom, we fulfill our highest calling: to know God intimately and to make His goodness known throughout the earth.

Salvation vs. Sanctification: The Ongoing Work of Freedom

Many believers have received salvation yet still struggle with areas of bondage. This is because while salvation is instantaneous—a moment of justification (just as if I never sinned) before God—sanctification is progressive. It is the daily process of being made holy, whole, and healed.

The tension between being "already saved" and "not yet fully free" is real. Paul expresses this paradox throughout his letters: we are seated with Christ in heavenly places (Ephesians 2:6), yet we are also urged to work out our salvation with fear and trembling

(Philippians 2:12). This tension is not a contradiction but an invitation—to apply the finished work of Christ to every area of life: mind, emotions, body, and will.

Sanctification is, in many ways, the unfolding of true freedom over a lifetime. It is not merely the absence of sin, but the presence of ever-increasing Christlikeness. Like the Israelites journeying through the wilderness after escaping Egypt, believers are invited to walk out their freedom step by step, trusting God to bring transformation in His timing and by His Spirit. While salvation delivers us from the penalty of sin, sanctification delivers us from its lingering power.

This journey requires both surrender and participation. The Holy Spirit empowers us to recognize patterns of thinking or behavior that still echo captivity—such as fear, unforgiveness, shame, or addiction. As we yield those areas to God and renew our minds with His truth, we begin to experience greater liberty. For example, someone may be saved yet feel paralyzed by guilt from their past. Through ongoing sanctification, the Holy Spirit gently reveals the roots of that shame and brings healing, replacing lies with the truth of God's love and acceptance.

Furthermore, sanctification is profoundly communal. It is lived out not in isolation, but within the body of Christ. Through relationships with other believers, accountability, encouragement, and prayer, we find support to persevere. The process is often gradual—like a sculptor patiently shaping raw stone into a masterpiece. Each day presents fresh opportunities to choose freedom over fear, faith over doubt, and love over resentment.

Ultimately, the journey of sanctification magnifies the generosity of God. He does not simply rescue us from darkness and leave us to fend for ourselves; He walks with us, shaping us into new creations. Our struggles and victories alike become testimonies of His grace, inviting others to discover the hope of true and lasting freedom.

Expanding our understanding of this journey helps us extend compassion to ourselves and others. We recognize that setbacks are not signs of defeat, but invitations to deeper trust. The ongoing work of sanctification is a testament to the patience and persistence of God, who is committed to seeing us flourish in the radiant, liberated life He designed.

As we embrace this process, we become living witnesses—embodying the freedom Christ offers and drawing others into the same redemptive story. In this way, salvation and sanctification together form the tapestry of spiritual freedom, moving us ever closer to the fullness of life in Christ.

Freedom Is More Than Emotional Relief

In our therapeutic culture, freedom is often reduced to emotional relief or the absence of stress. But biblical liberty goes far deeper. True freedom is the ability to align with God's truth and live it out. It empowers moral courage, fosters emotional stability, and grants spiritual authority. It is the inner wholeness that empowers outward obedience.

As Jesus said, "If the Son sets you free, you will be free indeed" (John 8:36). This "indeed" kind of freedom is comprehensive, touching every part of our lives—our thoughts, relationships, choices, and destinies.

Looking Ahead

In the chapters that follow, we'll explore how this divine freedom is modeled in the ministry of Jesus, revealed through the early Church, and made practical for believers today. Understanding this foundation—that God's design is for radiant, full-spectrum freedom— sets the stage for receiving and ministering deliverance with wisdom, confidence, and compassion.

Application Moment: Reflect, Repent, Respond

1. **Reflect**
   What stood out to you in this chapter?
   Example: "Have I embraced freedom as a process, not just a moment?"

2. **Repent**
   Are there any beliefs, habits, or wounds you sense God inviting you to surrender? *Example: "Lord, I repent for accepting fear as part of my identity."*

3. **Respond**
   What step can you take this week to move toward freedom?
   Example: "I will ask a trusted friend to pray with me as I break soul ties."

Chapter 2

JESUS, THE DELIVERER

To understand the full scope of deliverance and healing, we must look to the ultimate example: Jesus Christ. His ministry established a profound pattern, one that diverges in significant ways from the Old Testament understanding of "deliverance" yet sets the standard for all who would follow Him.

In the Old Testament, the concept of deliverance was intricately woven into the fabric of Israel's relationship with God, frequently manifesting as the removal of idolatry or the dramatic liberation from physical bondage, such as the famous exodus from Egypt. Deliverance was seen not only as rescue from external threats or captivity, but as a call to wholehearted allegiance to the one true God. Although the Old Testament contains no explicit accounts of exorcising evil spirits in the manner later revealed through Christ, it does portray freedom as being deeply connected to the eradication of false worship and the purification of both land and people from all that opposed God's holiness.

The spiritual leaders, including judges, prophets, and kings, were tasked with bringing the nation back to covenant faithfulness. This often meant physically tearing down altars and sacred pillars dedicated to foreign gods—act after act of courageous obedience in the face of social and spiritual compromise. For instance, in Exodus 34:13 and Deuteronomy 7:5, God's people are commanded to demolish the altars, break the sacred pillars, and burn the images of Canaanite deities. Passages such as Judges 2:2 and 6:25–35 recount the moments when figures like Gideon were called to destroy the altars of Baal, even when such actions risked family conflict or community outrage. Later, in the era of the kings, reformers such as Hezekiah and Josiah led national movements of repentance by purging the land of high places, Asherah poles, and other instruments of idol worship (2 Kings 18:4; 2 Kings 23:4–5, 8, 19–20).

These acts were more than symbolic—they represented a decisive turning away from spiritual bondage and a reclaiming of freedom under God's authority. Deliverance, then, was not just about removing surface-level threats but about reclaiming the heart. The process required courage, persistence, and a willingness to confront generations of compromise and syncretism. In every case, true liberty followed only when the people responded to God's call for holiness, tearing down the obstacles that clouded their devotion.

These Old Testament patterns of deliverance serve as prophetic foreshadowings of the more direct and personal freedom that would later be revealed in the ministry of Jesus Christ. Whereas ancient deliverance focused on uprooting external idols and purifying the community, Christ's coming would address the deepest internal strongholds, offering a holistic liberation— body, mind, and spirit. The groundwork laid by these ancient stories set the stage for the unique authority, compassion, and completeness of Christ's deliverance, as He engaged not only the physical but also the spiritual powers that hold humanity captive.

Jesus' model, however, presented a unified ministry of both healing and deliverance. The Gospels consistently show His work as integrated and holistic. For instance,

Luke 4:40-41 and 13:11-16 highlight how His ministry of healing and deliverance was interwoven.

> **40 When the sun was setting, all those who had any that were sick with various diseases brought them to Him; and He laid His hands on every one of them and healed them. 41 And demons also came out of many, crying out and saying, "You are the Christ, the Son of God!" And He, rebuking them, did not allow them to speak, for they knew that He was the Christ. Luke 4:40–41 (NKJV)**

> **"A woman had a spirit of infirmity eighteen years [...] Jesus said, 'Woman, you are loosed from your infirmity,' and she was made straight. But the Lord answered, 'Ought not this woman, being a daughter of Abraham, whom Satan has bound[...] for eighteen years, be loosed?'"— *Luke 13:11–16, NKJV (abridged)***

In fact, approximately one-third of Jesus' public ministry was dedicated to confronting demons and setting people free from their enslavement to the powers of darkness, alongside His healing work (Luke 13:31–32). He dealt directly with the "spirit in the man," often referred to by various terms like "demons, evil spirits, unclean spirits, [and] kinds of spirits." The Greek term *daimonizomai*, often incorrectly translated as "possessed," more accurately means "to be demonized," indicating a state of being influenced or afflicted rather than owned.[2] This demonstrates a continuing ministry, not an isolated set of events.

Jesus' encounters with demons were often dramatic. The Gadarene Demoniac, for example, was an extreme case, with every area of his life affected—socially, physically (cutting himself, tearing chains), emotionally, and mentally (crying aloud in torment). Yet, even in this state, the man retained a will and desire to be free. Many demons lived in him, with "Legion" acting as spokesman, revealing their fear of Jesus and their preference for inhabiting bodies. The pigs' berserk

---

[2] **Daimonizomai** (Greek: δαιμονίζομαι) is the primary New Testament verb used to describe individuals afflicted by demons. It occurs in passages like Matthew 8:28–34 and Mark 5:1–20. The term does not always denote full possession as in loss of control but often refers to varying degrees of **influence, torment, or oppression**. It emphasizes the **activity or operation of demons upon a person**—whether internally or externally—highlighting a spectrum of spiritual affliction. Strong, James. *Strong's Exhaustive Concordance of the Bible*, G1139. See also Vine, W.E. *Vine's Expository Dictionary of New Testament Words*, Nashville: Thomas Nelson, 1985, s.v. "Demon, Demon-Possessed."

stampede into the sea after the demons entered them demonstrated the entirely destructive nature of these spirits. Jesus expelled them with verbal commands, restoring the man to health and sanity, profoundly impacting the surrounding region.

> **"A certain man[...] had demons for a long time. He wore no clothes, nor did he live in a house but in the tombs. When he saw Jesus, he cried out... and said, 'What have I to do with You, Jesus, Son of the Most High God?'[...] For He had commanded the unclean spirit to come out[...] And they begged Him... Then the demons went out of the man and entered the swine, and the herd ran violently down the steep place[...]"— Luke 8:27–33, NKJV (abridged)**

The account of the child with an evil spirit further illustrates Jesus' approach. The disciples' inability to cast out the spirit highlighted their unbelief and failure to pray and fast. The boy's symptoms included seizures, muteness, and attempts by the demon to kill him by throwing him into water and fire. Jesus, discerning the "deaf and dumb spirit" through a word of knowledge, quickly performed the deliverance to avoid excess emotion and attention-craving from the demon.

In Capernaum, Jesus confronted an unclean spirit in the Jewish synagogue. This demonized man showed no prior symptoms, appearing as an ordinary person. Yet, Jesus' authority was so evident that the demon immediately manifested, shouting and fearfully acknowledging Jesus as "the Holy One of God." Jesus silenced the spirit and commanded it to leave, which it did with convulsions and shrieks but without harming the man. This public display powerfully demonstrated Jesus' unique authority over evil spirits. Even from a distance, Jesus could pronounce deliverance, as seen with the Syrophoenician woman's daughter, where the demon left the child when Jesus spoke miles away.

> **"In the synagogue, a man with an unclean spirit cried out, 'Let us alone! What have we to do with You [...] the Holy One of God!' But Jesus rebuked him, saying, 'Be quiet, and come out of him!' And the demon threw him in their midst... and came out without hurting him."— *Luke 4:33–35, NKJV***
>
> **"He said to her, 'For this saying go**

> **your way; the demon has gone out of your daughter.' And when she came to her house, she found the demon gone."** — *Mark 7:29–30, NKJV*

Jesus often healed demoniacs in large meetings. He would not allow demons to speak out, even as they became disruptive, shouting and shrieking upon departure. He also healed those "troubled by evil spirits," implying a lesser degree of demonic influence like affliction or oppression.

Jesus didn't just model this ministry; He commissioned His disciples to carry it on. This emphasis is clear throughout the New Testament: no one was sent out to evangelize without being commissioned to deal with evil spirits. He empowered the twelve disciples (Matthew 10:1-8) and the seventy (Luke 10:1, 17), giving them authority to cast out demons. This commission extended into the Great Commission itself (Mark 16:15-17; Matthew 28:19-20), ensuring that the apostolic continuation of deliverance ministry would be a core part of the Church's work. We see this actively demonstrated by Philip the evangelist in Acts 8:5-7, where unclean spirits cried out with loud voices and came out of many people, leading to great joy in the city.

The early Church continued this pattern. In Jerusalem, the community experienced rapid growth with harmony and healings. However, satanic activity quickly surfaced with Ananias and Sapphira, whose lie to the Holy Spirit led to their death, demonstrating the need for watchfulness to maintain spiritual ground. Satan struck back with severe persecution against the apostles, but as believers scattered, the proclamation of Jesus spread. Philip's simple proclamation of Christ in Samaria drove out demons, bringing restoration and healing.

The slave girl at Philippi, a fortune-teller exploited for financial gain, had a spirit of divination that recognized Paul and his companions (Acts 16:16-18). This demonic "word of knowledge" and distracting harassment was endured for days until Paul, taking authority in Jesus' name, commanded the spirit to leave. The immediate result was persecution, highlighting evil spiritual powers' hold on the culture, but the girl was freed. The Ephesian Revival saw the anointing manifest through cloths that touched Paul's body, causing sicknesses and demons to depart. Even when Jewish exorcists tried to invoke Jesus' name without true authority, they suffered humiliating public failure, further magnifying the name of Jesus (Acts 19:11-12; 13-16).

Throughout Acts, the Lordship of Jesus Christ was proclaimed, and demons were vanquished. Peter, Philip, Paul, and unnamed others demonstrated that demons must yield to disciples submitted to Christ's rulership. The Name of Jesus carries imperial authority, backed by legions of angels and the Godhead. This power equation is available to believers today.

The epistles, while not extensively portraying deliverance accounts, emphasize holy living as the means to keep demons out after conversion and baptism. Paul pictures believers in a "wrestling match" with invisible opponents—principalities, powers, rulers of darkness, and spiritual hosts of evil in high places (Ephesians 6:12). These are organized forces, from regional princes to "foot soldiers" establishing strongholds. We are born into this spiritual war zone and must fight with spiritual weapons, demolishing arguments and taking every thought captive to Christ (2 Corinthians 10:4-5). Watchfulness and holiness are essential to stay free, putting on the armor of light (Romans 13:12).

Application Moment: Reflect, Repent, Respond

1. **Reflect:**
   How does seeing Jesus as a Deliverer shape your relationship with Him? *Do you believe He is willing and able to deliver you today?*

2. **Repent:**
   Lay down any doubts, fears, or pride that keep you from surrendering fully to His healing work. *"Jesus, I repent for trusting in my own strength instead of Yours."*

3. **Respond:**
   Say aloud: *"Jesus, I invite You to be Deliverer in every area of my life."*

Chapter 3

UNMASKING THE ADVERSARY: UNDERSTANDING DEMONIC FORCES

To effectively engage in the ministry of deliverance, it is essential to understand what demons are and how they function. Scripture provides clarity—not only on their existence but also on their origin, nature, purpose, and operation in opposing God and tormenting humanity. This chapter pulls back the veil on these unseen adversaries, equipping you with foundational knowledge to confront them with confidence.

Defining the Enemy: Terminology and Identity

The New Testament uses precise language when addressing demonic forces, a clarity often lost in common parlance. The term "Devil" (Greek: *diabolos*) is a singular, personal title reserved exclusively for Satan, meaning "slanderer" or "accuser." He is the archenemy, the head of the kingdom of darkness. Demons, by contrast, are referred to with words like *daimonion*, *daimon*, or *pneuma akatharton*—"unclean spirits." These are subordinate spirits operating under Satan's authority. Referring to them in the plural as "devils" is both linguistically and theologically inaccurate, as it blurs the distinction between Satan and his legions.[3]

Jesus Himself identified Satan as "Beelzebub, the prince of demons" (Matthew 12:24), clearly establishing a hierarchy. The Apostle Paul further described him as "the prince of the power of the air" (Ephesians 2:2), signifying his influence over the spiritual atmosphere of the world. These evil spirits are disembodied and active, warring against believers,

---

[3] The term **"Devil"** (Greek: *diabolos*) appears as a singular noun in the New Testament, used exclusively for Satan. It means "slanderer" or "accuser," emphasizing his role as the chief adversary (e.g., Matthew 4:1; Revelation 12:10). In contrast, **"demons"** are identified by words such as *daimonion* (δαιμόνιον), *daimon* (δαίμων), or *pneuma akatharton*(πνεῦμα ἀκάθαρτον, "unclean spirit"), which refer to lesser spiritual beings under Satan's domain. Translating *daimonion* as "devils" (plural) is a linguistic and theological error that conflates Satan with his subordinate spirits. See: Vine, W. E. *Vine's Expository Dictionary of New Testament Words*, s.v. "Devil," "Demon." Also: Thayer, Joseph Henry. *Thayer's Greek-English Lexicon of the New Testament*. Grand Rapids: Baker Book House, 1977, pp. 122–124, 129–130.

influencing systems, cultures, and individuals. Just as angels operate under divine commission, demons function under rebellious orders in Satan's kingdom, driven by malice and destruction.

Their Ancient Fall: The Origin of Demonic Legions

The Bible outlines several stages in the fall and activity of demonic forces, tracing their rebellion back to antiquity. In the prophetic laments of Isaiah 14:12–15 and Ezekiel 28:12–19, we see the prideful fall of Lucifer, the "anointed cherub," who sought to exalt himself above God. His audacious rebellion resulted in his swift removal from heaven.[4]

---

[4] The fall of Lucifer is understood primarily through the prophetic imagery in **Isaiah 14:12–15** and **Ezekiel 28:12–19**, though both passages originally address the kings of Babylon and Tyre, respectively. Early Jewish and Christian tradition recognized these texts as containing **dual meanings**—referring to earthly rulers while simultaneously describing the supernatural rebellion of Satan, the "anointed cherub" who sought to exalt himself above the throne of God. His fall became emblematic of prideful rebellion and was later echoed in **Luke 10:18** where Jesus said, *"I saw Satan fall like lightning from heaven."* See: Pentecost, J. Dwight. *Things to Come*. Grand Rapids: Zondervan, 1958, pp. 378–382; Heiser, Michael S. *The Unseen Realm*, Bellingham, WA: Lexham Press, 2015, pp. 80–83; see also Gregory the Great, *Moralia in Job*, and early patristic commentary attributing these texts to Satan's fall.

ORIGIN OF DEMONS

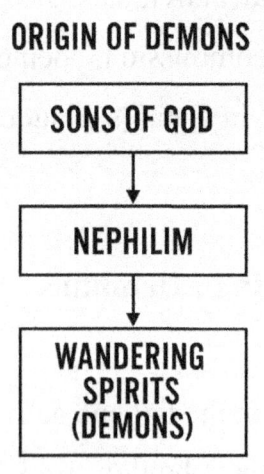

Revelation 12:3–4 further reveals that a third of the angelic host followed him in this rebellion, and they too were cast down from their exalted positions. These fallen angels are generally identified as demons, the primary inhabitants of Satan's kingdom. However, the Book of Jude (v. 6) introduces another layer to this understanding: "The angels who did not keep their proper domain... He has reserved in everlasting chains under darkness." This suggests that a subset of fallen angels are currently bound in judgment, while others remain active and free to carry out Satan's destructive agenda on earth.

Psalm 78:49 refers to a "band of evil angels" loosed by God in judgment, affirming their destructive agency in human affairs. Additionally, a debated but historically significant interpretation stems from Genesis 6:1–4, which describes the "sons of God" who cohabited with human women, producing a hybrid race known as the Nephilim. Many early Jewish sources—including the Book of Enoch (a text widely known and referenced in the ancient world, even by Jude)—assert that the disembodied spirits of these Nephilim became wandering demons, left without a physical home and constantly seeking to inhabit human bodies (cf. Matthew 12:43–45).[5] While the Nephilim interpretation is extra-biblical, these ancient texts reflect beliefs shared during Jesus' time and help explain the nature of certain demonic entities that crave embodiment.

Whether identified primarily as fallen angels or as the disembodied spirits of the Nephilim, the biblical and

---

[5] **Psalm 78:49** describes God releasing "a band of evil angels" (KJV: *"sending evil angels among them"*), affirming that even rebellious spirits may be used by God in judgment. The **Genesis 6:1–4** account of the "sons of God" and their union with the "daughters of men" has been interpreted by many early Jewish sources—including **1 Enoch, Jubilees**, and fragments from **Qumran (Dead Sea Scrolls)**—as referring to fallen angels (Watchers) who fathered a race of giants known as the **Nephilim**. According to *1 Enoch 15–16*, after the flood, the disembodied spirits of these giants became **roving demons**, cursed to wander the earth seeking habitation—an idea echoed in **Matthew 12:43–45**, where Jesus describes unclean spirits walking through "dry places." See: *The Book of Enoch*, trans. R.H. Charles. London: SPCK, 1917, ch. 15–16; Heiser, Michael S. *Demons: What the Bible Really Says About the Powers of Darkness*. Bellingham, WA: Lexham Press, 2020, pp. 71–91; Nickelsburg, George W.E. *1 Enoch: A Commentary on the Book of 1 Enoch, Chapters 1–36; 81–108*. Minneapolis: Fortress Press, 2001.

historical witness agrees on this crucial truth: demons are not fictional—they are real, personal, intelligent, and relentlessly destructive.

The Enemy's Agenda: Purpose and Activity

Demons operate with a singular, malevolent purpose, mirroring the destructive nature of their master, Satan. Their core agenda can be summarized in three primary aims:

- **To Deceive:** They are masters of illusion, actively promoting false doctrines, distorting truth, and entangling human hearts in lies. As 1 Timothy 4:1 warns, "In latter times some will depart from the faith, giving heed to deceiving spirits and doctrines of demons." They sow seeds of doubt and confusion, subtly leading people astray from God's clear truth.

- **To Afflict:** Their aim is to cause suffering, tormenting individuals physically, mentally, and emotionally. Luke 13:11–16 provides a vivid example of "a woman... who had a spirit of infirmity eighteen years[...] whom Satan has bound." This shows their capacity to inflict prolonged physical and emotional pain.

- **To Destroy:** Their ultimate goal aligns perfectly with Satan's declaration: "to steal, kill, and destroy" (John 10:10). They seek to ruin lives, relationships, and destinies. Their operations range from overt, dramatic manifestations (e.g., convulsions, audible voices, physical violence) to subtle, unseen bondage (e.g., cycles of perversion, chronic fear, unforgiveness, self-hatred). They are strategic and often embed themselves in generational curses, soul ties, and ungodly belief systems, making their influence deeply entrenched.

Wisdom from the Ancients: Early Church Testimony and Authority

The early Church was no stranger to demonic activity; indeed, confronting it was a natural part of their ministry, flowing directly from Jesus' commission. The writings of the early Church Fathers consistently affirm the existence and influence of demons, integrating deliverance into their understanding of Christian life and practice.

- **Justin Martyr** (c. 100–165 AD) wrote of demons trembling at the very name of Jesus, acknowledging His supreme authority.

- **Tertullian** (c. 155–220 AD) described how ordinary Christians could drive them out, not through elaborate incantations, but simply by invoking Christ's authority.

- **Irenaeus** (c. 130–202 AD) and **Origen** (c. 185–254 AD) both affirmed the continuity of this authority in the Church, highlighting that deliverance was a normal part of the Christian experience.

- The **Desert Fathers**, especially **Antony the Great** (c. 251–356 AD), were renowned for their spiritual warfare, actively engaging demons through fasting, Scripture meditation, solitude, and intercession.

Perhaps most tellingly, even baptismal rites in the early Church included formal renunciation of Satan and his demons, demonstrating that deliverance was integrated into discipleship—a foundational step in a believer's walk with Christ, not a specialized, fringe ministry.[6]

Empowered for Battle: Practical Understanding for the Church Today

Understanding what demons are is only the beginning—we must also understand how they gain access. Demons are legalistic entities. They exploit spiritual breaches: unrepented sin, unhealed trauma, unforgiveness, idolatry, generational iniquity, or willful participation in occult practices (as discussed in Chapter 6). They

---

[6] The early Church saw deliverance as a normal function of Christian ministry, rooted in Christ's authority over demonic forces. **Justin Martyr** (*Second Apology*, ch. 6) wrote of demons being cast out "by men everywhere and in every land, using the name of Jesus Christ." **Tertullian** asserted in *Apologeticus* (ch. 23) that even lay Christians could drive out demons through prayer and faith in Christ. **Irenaeus**, in *Against Heresies* (Book 2, ch. 32), affirmed that the Church continued Christ's ministry of casting out demons. **Origen**, in *Contra Celsum* (Book 1, ch. 46), taught that the name of Jesus held real power over demonic forces. The **Desert Fathers**, such as **Antony the Great**, exemplified rigorous spiritual disciplines as means of confronting demonic resistance (cf. *Life of Antony* by Athanasius, chs. 5–13). Baptismal liturgies in the early Church—particularly in the writings of **Cyril of Jerusalem** (*Catechetical Lectures*, II.4–5)—included renunciations of Satan and his works, formalizing deliverance as a prerequisite to initiation into Christian life.

function like spiritual squatters, seizing any area of a person's life not fully surrendered to Christ. This is not merely doctrinal knowledge; it is profoundly personal and pastoral.

I once ministered to a young man with a profound prophetic calling on his life. Even from childhood, the hand of God was unmistakable upon him. Yet as he matured and began to embrace that call, he was met with intense spiritual resistance. The oppression escalated until he was eventually committed to a psychiatric hospital, tormented and misunderstood by medical professionals who could only address his symptoms.

Through prayer and discernment, the Holy Spirit revealed multiple legal access points in his life: perversion, pornography, bitterness, deep-seated abandonment, and rejection. These open doors allowed demonic forces to torment his mind, emotions, and spirit, hindering his destiny. The deliverance wasn't instantaneous. It required weeks of intercession, fasting, counseling, and deliberate confrontation in the Spirit. But one by one, the oppressive spirits lost their grip. Today, this young man is not only free—he is thriving in ministry, boldly declaring the Lordship of Christ and serving others with authority and compassion.

This is a powerful reminder: demonic bondage is real, but so is deliverance. And often, those with the greatest destiny attract the greatest opposition, precisely because the enemy seeks to derail God's plans. We are not fighting a losing battle. "The weapons of our warfare are not carnal but mighty in God for pulling down strongholds" (2 Corinthians 10:4). When the Church neglects this realm, we leave people vulnerable and bound. But when we engage it biblically and wisely, we become instruments of liberty, helping others walk into the fullness of their divine calling.

The Defeated Foe – Our Victorious Stand

Demons are not imaginary. They are intelligent, organized, and active agents of darkness, relentlessly pursuing their destructive agenda. But they are also defeated. Through Jesus Christ, we have been given supreme authority to bind, cast out, resist, and overcome every unclean spirit. Understanding their origin, nature, and tactics doesn't lead us to fear—it positions us for victory.

As you continue this journey into deliverance, remember: the same Spirit who raised Jesus from the dead now lives in you (Romans 8:11). The adversary may be invisible, but he is not invincible. Christ has triumphed over all the powers of darkness (Colossians 2:15) —and He has given that victory to His Church.

Looking Ahead

Having unmasked the adversary and understood their fundamental nature, our next step is to delve deeper into their specific behaviors. In Chapter 4: Characteristics of Demons, we will explore the distinct traits, strategies, and patterns of demonic activity, further sharpening our ability to discern and confront them.

Application Moment: Reflect, Repent, Respond

1. **Reflect:**
   What spiritual battles are affecting your daily life that may have unseen roots?
   Are you minimizing spiritual warfare or overly fearing it?

2. **Repent:**
   Ask God to forgive you for any open doors—
   knowingly or unknowingly opened to the
   enemy.
   *"Lord, I renounce any agreement I've made
   with the enemy, even in ignorance."*

3. **Respond:**
   Begin to keep a journal of moments when you
   notice patterns of oppression or
   discouragement.

Chapter 4

THE ENEMY'S PROFILE: UNDERSTANDING DEMONIC CHARACTERISTICS

To effectively confront the works of darkness, the believer must not only understand what demons are (as explored in Chapter 3) but also how they function. Demons are not impersonal forces or mere concepts of evil; they are intelligent, personal spiritual beings with defined characteristics, malevolent goals, and predictable patterns of behavior. Knowing their traits allows us to discern their presence, understand their strategies, and resist them with biblical authority, rather than operating in ignorance or fear.

Beyond the Shadows: Unveiling Demonic Traits

Demons are not amorphous entities; they possess distinct attributes that govern their actions and interactions. Understanding these characteristics is crucial for effective spiritual warfare.

The Mind Behind the Malice: Demonic Personality

Unlike inanimate objects or abstract forces, demons demonstrate genuine personality. They possess **will** (Matthew 12:44), capable of making decisions and seeking specific outcomes. They exhibit **emotion** (James 2:19), trembling at the thought of God. And they possess **intellect** (Mark 1:24; Acts 19:15), allowing them to speak, reason, and strategize. Their capacity for knowledge enables them to manipulate situations and people effectively. Consider the chilling encounter with the Gadarene demoniac (Mark 5:6–13): the demons knew Jesus by name, they begged Him, they negotiated terms of departure, and they identified themselves collectively as "Legion"—a name that speaks volumes about their awareness of hierarchy, identity, and territory. This reveals a chilling intelligence at work.

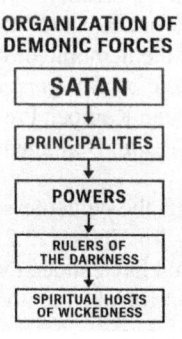

ORGANIZATION OF DEMONIC FORCES

SATAN

PRINCIPALITIES

POWERS

RULERS OF THE DARKNESS

SPIRITUAL HOSTS OF WICKEDNESS

Invisible Battlefronts: Territorial and Organized Influence

The demonic realm is not chaotic; it is highly organized, mirroring a dark military structure. Demons often attach themselves to specific regions, cultures, families, or individuals, seeking to establish dominion. Daniel 10:13 reveals that the **"Prince of Persia,"** a territorial spirit who resisted angelic messengers, highlighting a high-ranking demonic power assigned to a specific nation.[7] Jesus also references unclean spirits walking through "dry places" seeking rest (Matthew 12:43–45), suggesting that spiritual geography matters and that demons seek established "habitations."[8] Paul's powerful revelation in Ephesians 6:12 speaks of our wrestling match against "principalities, powers, rulers of darkness, and spiritual hosts of wickedness," indicating

---

[7] The concept of a **structured hierarchy among demonic forces** is biblically supported and has been consistently affirmed in Christian theology. **Daniel 10:13** references the *"Prince of the kingdom of Persia"* who withstood the angel Gabriel for 21 days, until Michael, *"one of the chief princes,"* came to help. This passage is widely interpreted as describing **territorial or geopolitical spirits**—high-ranking demons assigned to oppose God's purposes in specific regions or governments. Paul reinforces this notion in **Ephesians 6:12**, listing *"principalities, powers, rulers of the darkness of this world, and spiritual wickedness in high places"* as ranks within the demonic order. See: Unger, Merrill F. *Biblical Demonology: A Study of the Spiritual Forces Behind the Present World Unrest.* Wheaton: Van Kampen Press, 1952, pp. 141–147; Heiser, Michael S. *The Unseen Realm.* Bellingham, WA: Lexham Press, 2015, pp. 227–235.

[8] In Jewish tradition, "dry places" were associated with the wilderness—believed to be the dwelling of unclean spirits (cf. Lev. 16:10; Isa. 13:21–22; Tobit 8:3; 1 Enoch 10:4–6). Jesus' audience would have understood this imagery as demonic beings roaming lifeless, God-forsaken regions, seeking reentry into human hosts.

a layered and organized demonic hierarchy that influences earthly systems and societies.

The Restless Hunger: Craving Embodiment

One of the most striking characteristics of demons is their insatiable craving for a physical host. Without a body, demons are restless and uncomfortable, constantly seeking a physical dwelling place (Luke 11:24–26). They seek to inhabit people, animals (as seen with the swine in Mark 5:11–13), or even objects used in idolatry (Deuteronomy 7:25–26). Embodiment allows them to manifest their will, amplify torment, and express their destructive nature in the physical realm. When Jesus expelled demons, they often sought refuge in other

In Jesus' day, many understood that unclean spirits were restless without a body. Ancient Jewish writings, such as 1 Enoch, describe these spirits as wandering in "dry places" until they find a host. This host could be a person, an animal, or even an object used in idol worship.
That's why in the Gospels, after Jesus cast them out, demons often pleaded to enter another host—like the pigs in Mark 5:11–13—rather than remain disembodied (Matthew 12:43–45)

physical hosts, demonstrating this deep-seated need.[9]

Ranks of Darkness: Varying Power and Resistance

Not all demons are equal in strength or influence. The demonic realm mirrors military rank and structure, with varying levels of power and authority. Jesus Himself noted that 'this kind' (referring to a particularly stubborn spirit) only comes out by intense prayer and intentional fasting (Mark 9:29), indicating that certain spirits are more resistant and require greater spiritual force to dislodge. The encounter in Acts 19:13–16, where a single demon-possessed man overpowered seven sons of Sceva, dramatically revealed the strength and cunning of even individual demonic entities, highlighting the varying degrees of power within their hierarchy.

Targeted Attacks: Specialization in Assignment

Demons often function with specific assignments, specializing in particular areas of influence or affliction.

---

[9] See *1 Enoch* 15:8–16:1; *Tobit* 8:3; and Craig S. Keener, *The IVP Bible Background Commentary: New Testament*(Downers Grove, IL: InterVarsity Press, 1993), 72–73, for ancient Jewish perspectives on disembodied spirits and their quest for embodiment.

They can often be identified by name or by the manifestation they consistently produce. For example, Scripture speaks of a "spirit of infirmity" (Luke 13:11), a "spirit of fear" (2 Timothy 1:7), a "lying spirit" (1 Kings 22:22), or a "deaf and dumb spirit" (Mark 9:25). These names reflect their precise function and help the discerning believer identify them during ministry. Some operate primarily through emotional triggers, others through sexual sin, addiction, idolatry, or specific forms of deception. This specialization allows for targeted spiritual warfare.

The Scars They Leave: Causing Mental, Emotional, and Physical Harm

The ultimate goal of demonic activity is to inflict harm, and they do so across the entire spectrum of human experience:

- **Mental Torment:** Demons may influence compulsive behavior, irrational fears, deep depression, suicidal ideation, or even personality fragmentation (Mark 5:2–5). They whisper lies, sow confusion, and seek to distort perception.

- **Emotional Anguish:** They may aggravate existing emotional wounds, fueling shame, rejection, bitterness, chronic fear, or uncontrollable rage (2 Timothy 1:7). They thrive on unresolved pain and negative emotions.

- **Physical Affliction:** Scripture records numerous instances where demons caused physical ailments, including muteness (Matthew 9:33), blindness (Matthew 12:22), violent seizures (Mark 9:17–22), physical deformity (Luke 13:11–13), and various forms of pain. While it's crucial to remember that not all illness is demonic, some clearly are, and deliverance can bring profound physical healing.

Trembling Before Truth: Recognizing Jesus' Authority

Despite their power and malice, demons are not sovereign. They are acutely aware of who Jesus is (Mark 1:24) and they profoundly fear the authority given to His followers (Luke 10:17). They know their time is limited (Matthew 8:29) and their ultimate judgment is sealed (Revelation 20:10). James writes, "Even the demons believe—and tremble" (James 2:19). This knowledge, however, is not salvific or redemptive; it is a fear-induced recognition of a superior power.

The Return and Escalation: When Demonic Forces Revisit

A critical characteristic of demons, and a sobering warning from Jesus, is their tendency to return with greater force if the spiritual 'house' is left empty after expulsion. Jesus' warning in Matthew 12:43–45 outlines how a clean but empty vessel can become a worse habitation than before, as the spirit returns with seven more wicked spirits. This underscores the profound importance of filling the void after deliverance with the Holy Spirit's presence, God's Word, prayer, fellowship, and continuous submission to God.

Wolves in Sheep's Clothing: Deception and Masquerade

Demons are masters of disguise. 2 Corinthians 11:14 warns that Satan himself masquerades as an "angel of light," and his

> **And no wonder! For Satan himself transforms himself into an angel of light.**
> **2 Corinthians 11:14**

servants likewise masquerade as servants of righteousness. Demons may mimic genuine spiritual gifts, bring counterfeit visions, or even impersonate deceased loved ones to deceive and gain influence. They often exploit human emotion, sentimentality, or a desire for spiritual experiences to gain trust and lead people astray. Familiar spirits, in particular, prey on sentimentality, appearing during times of grief or in spiritualistic contexts to offer false comfort or guidance.

Final Reflection

Demons are strategic, intelligent, and driven by an agenda to oppose God's work and humanity's freedom. Yet believers are not helpless. By understanding their characteristics, recognizing their tactics, and applying Christ's authority, we walk in victory. Discernment, Scripture, and the indwelling Holy Spirit are our

41

indispensable tools for freedom and effective ministry. Jesus came to destroy the works of the devil (1 John 3:8), and we are called to continue this work—empowered, equipped, and fearless.

Looking Ahead

Having understood the fundamental characteristics of demonic forces, our next step is to delve into their operational strategies and the specific ways they gain access to lives. In **Chapter 5: The Enemy's Playbook – Tactics of Demonic Influence**, we will explore their core methods of attack, and then in **Chapter 6: Open Doors and Legal Ground – How Demons Gain Access**, we will uncover the vulnerable points they exploit.

Application Moment: Reflect, Repent, Respond

1. **Reflect:**
   Do any of the demonic traits described feel familiar in your life or family history?
   Which patterns seem persistent or cyclical?

2. Repent:

Break agreement with any traits (fear, lust, anger, etc.) you've tolerated.

"I reject and renounce every trait that does not align with the Spirit of God."

3. Respond:

Share what you're learning with a trusted friend or mentor and ask for accountability in prayer.

Chapter 5

THE ENEMY'S PLAYBOOK –
TACTICS OF DEMONIC
INFLUENCE

Have you ever felt a subtle pull towards something you knew was wrong, a persistent whisper of doubt, or a sudden, irrational surge of fear? These aren't always random occurrences. In the unseen realm, a ceaseless conflict rages, and demonic entities are far from passive. Their very existence is defined by their relentless opposition to God's purposes and their tireless efforts to keep humanity in bondage. To truly walk in the radiant freedom Christ offers and to effectively minister deliverance to others, we must first understand how these unseen adversaries operate—their stealthy tactics—and where they gain access. This chapter unveils the enemy's strategic tactics, empowering you to discern their schemes and stand firm against their influence.

The Deceitful Dance: Core Operational Methods of Demonic Spirits

Demons are master strategists, employing a range of deceptive tactics to exert control and inflict harm. Their activities are not always dramatic; often, they are subtle, weaving themselves into the fabric of our thoughts, emotions, and desires. Their methods can be broadly described by these distinct forms of attack:

- **Entice:** Imagine a lure, almost imperceptible, drawing you towards a forbidden desire or a subtle compromise. This is how demons entice—they woo, seduce, coerce, or tempt, a process distinctly different from the Holy Spirit's gentle guidance. It's the subtle whisper that makes ungodly desires seem appealing.

- **Deceive:** They are masters of illusion, actively distorting truth and promoting lies. They influence bad decisions by exaggerating problems, planting seeds of doubt, and subtly moving people away from God's unwavering truth. Paul warns that they can even blind people to spiritual realities, keeping them from seeing the light of the Gospel (2 Corinthians 4:4).

- **Enslave:** Their ultimate goal is to chain people up, making them captive and turning them into puppets, stripping away their God-given free will. This is tragically evident in patterns of compulsive behavior, relentless addictions, and obsessions that seem impossible to break.

- **Torment:** This is a cruel and pervasive tactic. Torment can manifest as physical pain (like chronic arthritis that defies medical explanation), mental anguish (such as the chilling fear of going insane or persistent suicidal ideation), or spiritual torment (like the gnawing fear of having committed the unforgivable sin). A chilling truth is that unforgiveness, a choice we make, is explicitly identified as an open door to such torment (Matthew 18:34–35).

- **Drive/Compel:** Think of the Gadarene demoniac, driven by unseen forces to live among tombs, cutting himself and tearing apart chains. Demons use irrational fears and relentless pressure to force people into certain behaviors.

Individuals can become so addicted, so consumed, that they feel compelled to repeat destructive actions, losing all sense of control (Mark 5:1–20; Luke 8:26–39; Matthew 8:28–34).

- **Defile:** They seek to corrupt what is pure and good. Through sin patterns and close association with darkness, they defile individuals, leaving a stain on their spirit and soul.

- **Oppose:** Demons are active adversaries. They stand directly against God's will and relentlessly resist the advancement of His Kingdom in individuals and throughout the world (Matthew 13:19; 2 Corinthians 4:4).

- **Pervert:** They are masters of distortion, twisting and corrupting what is inherently good and God-given, turning it to evil purposes (1 Thessalonians 2:18).

- **Possess:** In the most extreme and visible cases, a human being becomes a vessel. Here, the person does not display their true nature but that of the ruling spirit, losing significant control over their will and actions.

- **Teach:** These are the "deluding and seducing spirits" that whisper false doctrines, conveying falsehoods that subtly draw believers into error and away from sound teaching (1 Timothy 4:1 AMP). History is replete with examples, from the angel Moroni of Mormonism to the deceptive rites of various secret societies.

- **Make People Sick and Infirm:** While we must always affirm that not all illness is demonic, Scripture clearly shows instances where evil spirits can create specific physiological, psychological, and emotional weaknesses. Jesus' ministry often involved casting out spirits that caused physical infirmities (Luke 13:11 AMP).

Beneath all these tactics, there's a consistent thread: demons relentlessly fight against **peace** in every aspect of life: inner personal harmony, peace of mind, physical well-being, harmonious relationships, and a harmonious adjustment to external circumstances. The great distinctive mark of demonic activity is **restlessness**. When a life or situation is persistently devoid of true peace and characterized by agitation, it signals a high probability of demonic influence.

The Battle Lines: Two Positions of Demonic Operation

Understanding where a demon is operating from dictates how a believer responds. There are two primary positions of demonic influence:

- **From Outside the Body:** Imagine a prowling lion, seeking whom it may devour (1 Peter 5:8). In this scenario, demons are external tempters, external pressures, or influences seeking to gain entry. When they operate from outside, believers are called to **resist** them. "Submit yourselves, then, to God. Resist the devil, and he will flee from you" (James 4:7). This applies to general temptations, external pressures, or influences subtly trying to gain a foothold.

- **From Within the Body:** If a demon has found an "open door" and established a deeper level of influence or affliction within a person, they are operating from within. In such cases, believers are empowered to **expel** them. Jesus

49

demonstrated this repeatedly, casting out spirits with a word (Matthew 8:16; Mark 1:39).

Looking Ahead

Having explored the strategic tactics and operational positions of demonic spirits, our next step is to understand *how* they gain access to lives. In **Chapter 6: Open Doors and Legal Ground – How Demons Gain Access**, we will uncover the specific vulnerabilities and entry points that allow the enemy to establish a foothold.

Application Moment: Reflect, Repent, Respond

1. **Reflect:**
   Which of the enemy's tactics have been effective in your life—distraction, deception, discouragement, etc.?
   How has this affected your spiritual health and relationships?

2. **Repent:**
   Confess areas where you've allowed the enemy's lies to shape your beliefs.
   "God, I choose truth over deception, light over darkness."

3. **Respond:**
Memorize one Scripture that counters a lie you've been believing and speak it daily this week.

Chapter 6

OPEN DOORS AND LEGAL GROUND – HOW DEMONS GAIN ACCESS

In the spiritual realm, demons do not operate arbitrarily; they are not simply random attackers. They meticulously seek 'legal ground' or 'entry points' through which they can establish influence and exert control in a person's life. Understanding these common gateways is critical for both receiving and resisting deliverance, as these vulnerabilities act like magnets, drawing oppressive and deceptive tactics. This chapter will illuminate these vulnerable points, empowering you to identify and close any open doors in your life.

The Vulnerable Points: Gateways to Influence

Demons exploit specific areas of vulnerability, sin, or exposure that grant them permission, or "legal ground," to operate.

The Senses as Portals: Eye, Ear, and Mouth Gates

Our senses are powerful portals. What we choose to consume, hear, and speak can either fortify our spiritual defenses or create dangerous breaches in our "moral 'walls' of protection" (Proverbs 25:28).

- **Eye Gate:** Consistently viewing ungodly media, such as sexually immoral movies or pornographic content, is like leaving the city gates wide open. It "opens the 'Eye Gate' of his or her walled city and makes it easy for evil spirits to come in," inviting spirits of lust or adultery to take up residence.
- **Ear Gate:** Similarly, deliberately listening to unwholesome music, gossip, or conversations that are unedifying can provide an open invitation for evil spirits to implant thoughts and influences.

- **Mouth Gate:** Our words carry power. Ungodly verbal output, such as gossip, slander, blasphemy, or constant negativity, can also create spiritual vulnerabilities. Demons can then find residence in these parts of our lives, influencing our thoughts, emotions, and even our physical bodies through what we allow ourselves to say.

Forbidden Paths: Occult Practices and False Religions

These constitute direct and profoundly dangerous open doors to demonic influence, deliberately seeking contact with the supernatural realm outside of Christ. History, and indeed our current times, is "filled with the occult and false religions."

- **Engagement with the Supernatural Apart from Christ:** Any activity that attempts to gain spiritual power, knowledge, or influence apart from Jesus Christ falls into this category. This includes séances, playing with Ouija boards, engaging in divination (fortune-telling, clairvoyance, horoscopes, astrology, consulting mediums, necromancy), or participating in witchcraft (spells, curses, hexes, hypnosis). God explicitly and repeatedly prohibits such practices, warning of severe consequences (Deuteronomy 18:9-14).

- **Modern Manifestations:** This extends to seemingly benign forms of "meditation" that open the mind to ungodly spiritual influences, oriental cults and philosophies (e.g., certain forms of yoga focused on spiritual connection outside of Christ), and the belief in reincarnation.

- **Consequences:** The presence of occult spirits can be reinforced by disturbing manifestations in a person's life, such as recurring nightmares, hearing noises or voices, or seeing unsettling images.

- **Closing the Door:** To truly close these doors, it's not enough to simply stop the practice. One must actively **renounce** all involvement and, crucially, actively **destroy** associated amulets, books, and objects. As Acts 19:19 demonstrates, this physical act of severing ties is vital, "lest the spirits have a portal of entry into your home or your life." This intentional breaking of contact prevents re-entry points and reinforces spiritual boundaries.

Wounds from the Past: Trauma and Childhood Exposure

The tender years of childhood, and indeed even the womb, can create profound vulnerabilities that become starting points for demonic issues. These experiences can deeply wound the soul, creating entry points that persist into adulthood.

- **Sudden Shock/Abandonment:** "Death-dealing spirits" may enter due to "sudden shock, such as when an angry parent gives a child a very harsh verbal scolding or abandons the child as a means of discipline." Such moments leave deep emotional scars.
- **Parental Disharmony:** A home filled with disharmony and strife between parents in a child's early life can expose them to demonic influences, as peace is consistently fought against.

- **Early Life Impact:** The sobering truth that "Most demonic issues start as early as the womb – 5 years old" highlights the profound and lasting impact of early life experiences on spiritual vulnerability.

Inherited Vulnerabilities: Generational Sin and Ungodly Soul Ties

These are powerful gateways that can extend influence across family lines, impacting individuals through no fault of their own, yet requiring their active participation to break free.

- **Generational Iniquity:** Patterns of unrighteousness, sin, or idolatry can be passed down through family lines, creating a predisposed openness for certain demonic influences (Exodus 20:5). It's a spiritual inheritance of vulnerability.

- **Unholy Soul Ties:** These are deep, often unhealthy, emotional or sexual bonds formed particularly through illicit sexual relationships or controlling emotional connections. They act like an "umbilical cord" that needs to be broken, as they can provide legal ground for demons to operate. Such ties are frequently implicated in compulsive sexual aberration, described as demonic, and can be a form of self-hatred that "holds the door open wide to demonic invasion." Beyond sex, lusts and addictions (such as gluttony or alcohol dependence) are also key areas where these ties and demonic operations thrive.

The Enemy's Claim: Unforgiveness and Hidden Sin

These two internal conditions provide significant legal ground for demonic activity and severely weaken spiritual defenses, acting as breaches in our "moral walls" that the enemy eagerly exploits.

- **Unforgiving Heart:** An unforgiving heart creates a spiritual stronghold, blocking prayers and allowing tormenting spirits to retain their "legal right to torment" (Matthew 18:34–35). It's like leaving the door ajar for the very tormentor you wish to escape.

- **Unconfessed Sin:** Sinful acts or habits, especially when unconfessed and unrepented of, weaken an individual's spiritual defenses. They create a "moment or place of weakness"— whether emotional, physical, or a character failure. These deliberate and unrepentant sins can effectively "break a hedge" of protection, allowing a "serpent" (demon) to "bite" (Ecclesiastes 10:8). Sexual sin, in particular, is highlighted as a profoundly dangerous "hedge-breaking" act, leading to soul-level contamination and even demonic transference through sexual contact.

The Battle for Sustained Freedom: A Personal Story

There was a young woman in our ministry who, without question, was a Christian. I believe with full conviction that she was saved, blood-washed, and Spirit-filled. When she committed herself to the Lord, she would worship deeply, pray passionately, and walk in discernible spiritual strength. But as her walk intensified, so did the enemy's attacks.

Despite seasons of breakthrough—through fasting, prayer, and consecration—there remained a pattern. The moment she returned to certain environments, old companions, and familiar sins, she would slip back into cycles of bondage. Environments filled with lust, addiction, and spiritual compromise would reopen doors we had fought to close. Her battle was not just spiritual—it was environmental and relational.

This young woman's experience profoundly illustrates that deliverance requires not only casting demons out but also making hard decisions to stay out of the places where they wait to return. As long as she stayed consecrated, she was free. But proximity to old strongholds, ungodly soul ties, and familiar sins reopened wounds and provided fresh legal ground. We continue to pray for her full deliverance—because deliverance is not just an event. It's a lifestyle of intentional separation and spiritual discipline.

Demonic Activity in the Body of a Believer: Can a Christian Have a Demon?

Perhaps one of the most discussed and debated questions in deliverance ministry is: "Can a Christian have a demon?" While the Bible does not explicitly state, "Christians can have demons," it presents enough compelling evidence and principles that demand serious, honest consideration.

- **The Sanctification Process:** While salvation provides instantaneous justification—a moment of being declared righteous before God—sanctification is a progressive work. It's the daily process of being made holy, whole, and healed. This means that not every part of a believer's life is immediately and fully yielded to God's presence. There can be unyielded areas, unhealed wounds, or unconfessed sins.

- **Biblical Indication of "Filthiness":** The Bible commands believers to "cleanse themselves from all filthiness of the flesh and spirit" (2 Corinthians 7:1). This implies that "filthiness" (which can certainly include demonic influence

61

or residue) can still exist in the life of a Christian, requiring ongoing spiritual hygiene.

- **God's Omnipresence vs. Demonic Trespass:** The common argument, "How can the Holy Spirit and a demon live in the same house?" often assumes that God's omnipresence means immediate, complete expulsion of all darkness. However, God's omnipresence allows Him to be in a place even if other spirits are present. If demons are present in a believer, they are **trespassers on holy ground**—and they must be evicted through spiritual authority.

- **"Broken Hedges":** As Ecclesiastes 10:8 warns, "He who breaks a hedge, a serpent will bite him." This powerful image illustrates how sin, disobedience, or unaddressed wounds can tear down spiritual protection, allowing the enemy access. Jesus Himself referred to demons as "serpents and scorpions" (Luke 10:19), reinforcing this imagery of spiritual vulnerability.

- **The "Empty House" Principle:** Jesus' warning in Matthew 12:43-45 describes what happens when a demon is cast out and the "house" (a person's life) is left empty—it can return with seven more spirits worse than itself. This principle applies to believers: deliverance without subsequent infilling by the Holy Spirit and consistent spiritual discipline can tragically lead to deeper torment.

- **Defilement of God's Temple:** The Bible warns that even "God's temple" (our body, as believers) can be defiled (1 Corinthians 3:16–17). If defilement is possible, then demonic influence is indeed possible too.

It's crucial to understand that demonic oppression does not negate salvation. Christians can be saved, Spirit-filled, and still struggle with spiritual strongholds that require deliverance. The goal is not to instill fear or condemnation but to foster freedom through humility, repentance, and absolute dependence on the Holy Spirit. Deliverance is not about judgment—it is about Jesus' boundless mercy and His unwavering victory.

Recognizing Demonic Activity: The Absence of Peace and Presence of Restlessness

How can you tell if demonic activity is at play, whether from without or within? A critical key is its consistent fight against **peace** in every aspect of life. This includes inner personal harmony, peace of mind, physical well-being, harmonious relationships, and a harmonious adjustment to external circumstances. The great distinctive mark of demonic activity is **restlessness**. When a life or situation is persistently devoid of true peace and characterized by agitation, turmoil, or a nagging unease, it signals a high probability of demonic influence.

Equipping for Resistance and Expulsion

Understanding the specific operational methods of demons and the "legal ground" they exploit empowers believers to engage in targeted spiritual warfare. By identifying their tactics and actively closing the "open doors" through genuine repentance, radical forgiveness, and intentional holy living, individuals can significantly reduce demonic influence. Furthermore, recognizing that demons can operate as "trespassers" within a believer underscores the continuous need for spiritual hygiene and the courageous exercise of Christ's authority to resist them from outside and expel them from within. This foundational understanding lays bare the enemy's playbook and sets the stage for practical steps of deliverance and sustained freedom.

Looking Ahead

Now that we understand how demons gain access and how they can operate even in believers, we will next explore the specific names and functions of various demonic spirits. In **Chapter 7: Scriptural Names of Demonic Spirits**, we will sharpen our discernment by learning to identify the enemy more precisely.

Application Moment: Closing the Gates

1. **Reflect:**
   Which of the "open doors" listed—occult involvement, unforgiveness, trauma, generational sin, soul ties, or habitual sin— resonates with your personal experience? *Are there spiritual "gates" in your life that remain unguarded or unhealed?*

2. **Repent:**

   Ask the Holy Spirit to reveal specific entry points that need closing.

   "Lord, I repent for every sin, partnership, or behavior that gave the enemy legal ground in my life. I renounce them in Jesus' name."

3. **Respond:**

   Write down one known open door. Then, in prayer, **(1)** renounce it, **(2)** ask for cleansing by the blood of Jesus, and **(3)**declare that door closed.

   Example: "I renounce my involvement in astrology. I apply the blood of Jesus over that open door. I declare it permanently closed and sealed in Jesus' name."

Chapter 7

SCRIPTURAL NAMES OF DEMONIC SPIRITS

In the unseen spiritual realm, battles are often fought with precision. Just as a military commander identifies an enemy's unit, its capabilities, and its specific mission, so too can believers gain strategic insight by understanding the identities of demonic spirits. Beyond merely knowing *that* demons exist and *how* they operate, recognizing them by name, manifestation, and biblical context is essential for effective spiritual warfare. Scripture reveals that these entities, much like angels designated by function (e.g., Gabriel, the messenger), also operate under distinct roles and are often named after the kind of influence they exert. This chapter will delve into the specific identities of these unseen adversaries, arming you with knowledge for targeted, powerful prayer and deliverance.

Why Names Matter in Spiritual Warfare

In biblical thought, names are far more than mere labels; they represent function, authority, and essence. To know a name is to grasp its nature and often its power. In spiritual warfare, this principle holds profound significance:

- **Clarity and Precision:** Calling a spirit by its name and function brings clarity to the spiritual battle. It allows believers to move beyond vague prayers against "evil" to targeted, precise commands rooted in the believer's authority in Christ.

- **Jesus' Example:** Jesus frequently addressed demons by their specific behavior or title before casting them out. For instance, He asked the Gerasene demoniac, "What is your name?" and the reply was "My name is Legion" (Mark 5:9). He commanded the "deaf and mute spirit" directly (Mark 9:25). This demonstrates the power and purpose of identification.

- **Exposing Assignments:** Names often reveal a

spirit's specific assignment and expose the **entry points** it has exploited in a person's life. Knowing the "name" helps uncover the "game plan" of the enemy.

- **Asserting Authority:** When a believer, operating in the authority of Jesus Christ, names a spirit, it is an act of spiritual jurisdiction. It asserts Christ's Lordship over that specific influence, breaking its legal ground through the power of His blood.

Scriptural Names and Descriptions of Demonic Spirits

The Bible reveals various types of demonic spirits, often identified by their primary influence or the affliction they cause. Understanding these specific identities provides a framework for more effective discernment and ministry:

1. **Spirit of Infirmity (Luke 13:11):**
   - This spirit is directly associated with sickness and physical ailments. Jesus

encountered a woman who had been bent over for 18 years by a "spirit of infirmity."

- ○ **Operation:** While it's crucial to note that *not all illness is demonic*, some prolonged, mysterious, or medically unexplainable ailments may have spiritual roots linked to this spirit. It can cause chronic pain, physical deformities, or debilitating conditions.

2. **Deaf and Dumb Spirit (Mark 9:25):**

- ○ This spirit can inflict literal physical deafness and muteness, as seen in the boy Jesus delivered.

- ○ **Operation:** Beyond the physical, this spirit can also hinder people from hearing spiritual truth, understanding God's Word, or articulating their faith. It acts like "invisible earmuffs" that keep them spiritually ignorant, dulling spiritual hearing and expression.

3. **Unclean Spirit (Mark 1:23; Luke 11:24):**

   o This term is used over twenty times in the New Testament, making it a common designation for various defiling spirits.

   o **Operation:** Unclean spirits are associated with moral impurity, perversion, sexual sin, addiction, and rebellion against God's standards. They seek to defile individuals, relationships, and environments, often leading to compulsive behaviors or a sense of inner filthiness.

4. **Spirit of Blindness (Matthew 12:22; 2 Corinthians 4:4):**

   o This spirit is linked to both literal physical blindness and, more commonly, metaphorical spiritual inability to see or perceive truth.

   o **Operation:** It actively works to prevent people from "seeing" the light of the Gospel, understanding spiritual realities, or discerning God's will. It keeps individuals in darkness and deception.

5. **Familiar Spirit (Leviticus 20:27; Isaiah 8:19):**

   ○ These are counterfeit spirits that aim to deceive and mislead by imitating or impersonating deceased loved ones, or by providing information that seems supernaturally gained.

   ○ **Operation:** They often operate through mediums, necromancy (consulting the dead), or ancestral worship practices. Their goal is to lure people away from God's truth by offering false comfort or forbidden knowledge.

6. **Lying Spirit (1 Kings 22:22–23; 2 Chronicles 18:20–22):**

   ○ This spirit actively deceives prophets, leaders, and individuals, promoting falsehoods as truth.

   ○ **Operation:** It influences false visions, deceptive dreams, manipulative communication, and the belief in self-deception. It thrives on misinformation and confusion.

7. **Seducing Spirit (1 Timothy 4:1):**

   o These spirits subtly draw believers into doctrinal error, hyper-grace theology (which minimizes the need for holiness), legalism (which emphasizes works over grace), and spiritual elitism.

   o **Operation:** They operate heavily through false teachers and deceptive teachings, leading people astray from sound biblical doctrine and genuine faith.

8. **Foul Spirit (Mark 9:25; Revelation 18:2):**

   o Often synonymous with an unclean spirit, this term can also imply a particularly repulsive, aggressive, or violent manifestation.

   o **Operation:** It is marked by its offensive nature, often manifesting in outbursts of rage, violence, or extreme moral degradation.

9. **Jealous Spirit (Numbers 5:14, 30):**

   o This spirit stirs suspicion, irrational

relational conflict, and intense rivalry.

○ **Operation:** It can cause unfounded accusations, possessiveness, and destroy trust in relationships, leading to bitterness and isolation.

10. **Spirit of Divination (Acts 16:16):**

○ The Greek word here is *python*, linking it to the Python spirit of Delphi, known for its oracle.

○ **Operation:** It enables fortune-telling, clairvoyance, counterfeit prophecy, and other forms of occultic foretelling, offering false guidance and drawing people into forbidden spiritual practices.

11. **Spirit of Fear (2 Timothy 1:7; 1 John 4:18):**

○ This spirit brings torment, panic attacks, irrational dread, and phobias.

○ **Operation:** It directly opposes God's gifts of love, power, and sound thinking, paralyzing individuals with anxiety and preventing them from stepping into their divine purpose.

12. **Spirit of Heaviness (Isaiah 61:3):**

- ○ This spirit causes deep depression, despair, emotional exhaustion, and a sense of overwhelming burden.

- ○ **Operation:** It seeks to crush the human spirit, leading to lethargy and hopelessness. It is directly opposed by "the garment of praise," which brings joy and spiritual buoyancy.

Functional Demons Named by Manifestation

Beyond these explicitly named spirits, the Bible also refers to demonic spirits by the *manifestation* or *fruit* they produce in a person's life. These are often inferred from consistent patterns of behavior or character flaws that seem to have a spiritual root.

- • **Spirit of Pride:** Often associated with Lucifer's original sin (Isaiah 14), this spirit promotes self-exaltation, arrogance, and a refusal to submit to God or human authority. It blinds individuals to their own faults and hinders repentance.

- **Spirit of Lust:** Operates in sexual immorality, obsessive fantasy, and compulsive addiction. It perverts God's design for intimacy and leads to cycles of shame and bondage.

- **Spirit of Perversion:** This spirit twists truth, identity, and purity, leading to confusion about gender, sexuality, and moral boundaries. It seeks to distort God's original design in every area.

- **Spirit of Rebellion:** Directly opposes authority, fosters defiance, and refuses correction or submission. It can manifest as stubbornness, anarchy, and a constant urge to go against established order.

These functional names are not always explicitly stated in the Bible as distinct spirits but are powerful descriptors of how demonic influence can manifest, providing clarity for prayer and deliverance.

Broader Symbolic Descriptions of the Enemy

The Bible also uses powerful, symbolic imagery to

describe the overarching nature and influence of evil forces, particularly Satan himself and the systems he uses:

- **Lion (1 Peter 5:8):** Peter warns that "your enemy the devil prowls around like a roaring lion looking for someone to devour." This symbolizes Satan's predatory, intimidating, and destructive nature.

- **Dragon (Revelation 12:7–9):** The book of Revelation vividly portrays the devil as "the great red dragon," symbolizing his ancient power, ferocity, and his role as the accuser and persecutor of God's people.

- **Serpent (Genesis 3):** From the Garden of Eden, the serpent symbolizes the deceiver, cunning, subtle, and insidious in its temptation and corruption.

- **Beast (Revelation 13):** This symbol often represents anti-Christ systems, oppressive empires, or political powers that are empowered by Satan to wage war against God and His people.

These symbols reflect the nature of evil forces at work in both individual lives and broader societal systems, providing a macro-level understanding of the spiritual war.

The Power of Naming in Deliverance

In Scripture, Jesus frequently called out spirits by their behavior or title before casting them out. This practice is not about giving power to the demon but about exercising the authority of Christ over it. Naming the spirit, when led by discernment:

- **Exposes its Nature:** It brings the hidden work of darkness into the light, revealing the specific lie or bondage.

- **Asserts Authority:** It is a direct command, asserting the believer's God-given authority over that specific influence in Jesus' name.

- **Breaks its Legal Ground:** By identifying the spirit and the "door" it used, it facilitates the breaking of its legal right to operate through repentance and renunciation.

- **Brings Focus:** It helps the person receiving ministry to understand what they are being delivered from and to target their own repentance and resistance.

Discerning Spirits with Wisdom

While understanding these names is powerful, it is vital to approach deliverance with wisdom and discernment (as discussed in Chapter 13). Not every problem is caused by a demon, and not every struggle requires a named spirit to be cast out.

- **Balance:** Use biblical discernment, prayer, and Spirit-led insight before labeling a struggle. Is it the flesh, a natural issue, or truly a demonic influence?

- **Goal:** Remember that deliverance should always

lead to deeper intimacy with Christ, not just symptom relief. The goal is holistic freedom and a life lived in the fullness of God's Spirit.

Understanding the scriptural names and traits of demonic spirits arms believers with strategic insight for deliverance. These names are not merely labels but reveal tactics, influence, and assignments that can be dismantled through the authority of Jesus Christ. Targeted warfare brings deeper freedom and sustained victory, empowering believers to walk in the fullness of their inheritance.

Application Moment: Name It and Break It

1. **Reflect:**
   Which demonic identities or manifestations named in this chapter have shown up in your life or lineage—such as fear, infirmity, perversion, heaviness, or pride?
   Have you ever dismissed a persistent struggle as "just part of who I am" instead of naming it for what it is?

2. **Repent:**
   Ask the Holy Spirit to expose any hidden or disguised spirits influencing your thoughts, health, or emotions.
   "Father, forgive me for tolerating spirits that

oppose Your truth. I renounce every identity
that contradicts my identity in Christ."

3. **Respond:**
   Write down the name of one specific spirit
   you've identified (e.g., fear, lust, heaviness).
   Then pray aloud:
   "In the name of Jesus, I break agreement with
   the spirit of [name]. I command it to leave me
   now. Holy Spirit, fill every place that was
   previously occupied."

   Follow up with praise and declare a Scripture
   truth that directly counters that spirit (e.g., 2
   Timothy 1:7 for fear).

Chapter 8

SAVED... AND STILL IN CHAINS?

One of the most emotionally charged questions in deliverance ministry is this: Can a Christian have a demon?

To many, the question itself feels contradictory. We believe in the new birth, the indwelling of the Holy Spirit, and the finished work of Christ. How, then, could darkness cling to someone who belongs to the Light? Yet if you've walked closely with people-listened to the stories of sincere, Spirit-filled believers trapped in cycles of fear, compulsion, torment, or infirmity-you know this isn't just theoretical. It's personal, pastoral, and urgent.

I once held the common assumption: A Christian can't possibly have a demon. Then I met people who loved Jesus, worshiped deeply, and yet were undeniably tormented. Under Christ's authority, they received deliverance-and their lives changed.

Ministers like Derek Prince have long testified to this reality: the question isn't whether believers belong to Christ (they do), but whether parts of their lives can still be occupied by spiritual enemies that need to be evicted.

This chapter approaches the topic with care. It neither sensationalizes nor minimizes. It invites us to hold two biblical truths together: we are fully Christ's-and we are still being made fully whole.

Clearing the Language: Possession vs. Oppression

Before we explore how demonic influence operates, it's important to clarify the language often used in spiritual discussions. Understanding the difference between possession and oppression lays the foundation for a biblical perspective on deliverance.

The confusion is largely linguistic. In everyday English, *possession* suggests total ownership and control. In the New Testament, the Greek verb *daimonizomai* is frequently used and is more accurately translated as "to be demonized" or "to be under demonic influence." This term suggests varying degrees of harassment or control by demonic forces, without implying that the person is legally owned by a demon.

While many theologians distinguish between demonic oppression and possession, some argue that applying the term "demonized" to a Christian is still not biblically sound. This chapter maintains that the term accurately describes the spiritual harassment that is possible, while firmly upholding Christ's legal ownership of the believer.

Scripture is unambiguous about ownership:

> **"You are not your own, for you were bought with a price; therefore glorify God in your body and in your spirit, which are God's." (1 Corinthians 6:19–20)**

The believer's spirit is the dwelling place of the Holy Spirit and bears His seal. Demons cannot own what Christ has purchased. Yet the same Scriptures acknowledge that Christians can be:

- **Oppressed** (harassed from without)
- **Afflicted** (tormented in mind, emotion, or body)
- **Influenced** (deceived or manipulated where

ground has been given)

Jesus freed a daughter of Abraham—clearly part of God's covenant people—who had been bound for eighteen years. Paul warns believers not to "give place to the devil" (Ephesians 4:27) and calls us to "cleanse ourselves from all filthiness of the flesh and spirit" (2 Corinthians 7:1). We are justified, yes—but we are also being sanctified. That tension explains why ongoing spiritual conflict can remain even after genuine conversion.

Breaking the Hedge: How Doors Open

With a clearer understanding of spiritual terminology, we now turn to the question of access. How do these spiritual influences find entry points into the lives of believers?

Ecclesiastes 10:8 paints a stark picture:

> **"He who breaks a hedge, a serpent will bite him."**

In the ancient world, hedges and walls kept predators and thieves at bay. Spiritually, the hedge is formed by obedience, holiness, and alignment with God's Word. Sin creates breaches; the serpent exploits them.

Jesus Himself uses serpent and scorpion imagery for demonic powers. The point is not to frighten but to warn: *wherever a breach is tolerated, vulnerability remains.*

Few breaches cut as deeply as sexual sin. Paul writes:

> **"He who sins sexually sins against his own body,"** **directly defiling the very temple meant for the Spirit's presence (1 Corinthians 6:18).**

Deliverance ministers have long observed that sexual immorality—especially when entangled with occult practices, addiction, or trauma—can function as a gateway for unclean spirits. In pagan rites and occult initiations, sexual acts are intentionally used to break moral resistance, fracture the soul, and invite spiritual bondage.

Where breaches have formed, they can be healed through repentance, deliverance, and the renewing work of the Holy Spirit.

Demonic Gateways: How the Enemy Gains Access

To understand how spiritual breaches manifest, it is helpful to examine the specific gateways through which, according to some Christian traditions, demonic influences might gain access. These gateways are often understood as overlapping, contributing to multiple layers of spiritual vulnerability. Importantly, perspectives on these ideas can vary widely across denominations and theological schools of thought.

The term "legal ground" refers to the belief—held among many in the deliverance and spiritual warfare traditions—that certain actions, mindsets, or unresolved issues grant spiritual entities permission to influence a person's life. This concept is often drawn from passages like Ephesians 4:27, which warns, "do not give the devil a foothold." While not all Christian traditions use this language, the idea is that persistent sin or willful disobedience can create opportunities for spiritual oppression.

One significant entry point involves what some call the Eye, Ear, and Mouth "gates." In this view, what we see, hear, and speak can either strengthen our spiritual defenses or create vulnerabilities. For example, regularly consuming media that is sexually immoral is thought to open the "Eye Gate," potentially inviting spiritual oppression related to lust. This interpretation flows from verses like Matthew 6:22-23, where Jesus teaches on the eye as "the lamp of the body."

Engaging in occult practices or participating in occultic religious rituals is widely regarded—across many Christian traditions—as a direct spiritual danger. Activities such as séances, use of Ouija boards, or divination are prohibited in Deuteronomy 18:10-12, which calls such practices "detestable." Some believers understand that objects linked to these practices can act as "doorways," and so they are often destroyed or removed as part of spiritual cleansing rituals. Others may approach these warnings as cultural protections rather than direct spiritual mechanisms.

When discussing "soul ties," it is important to define the term: many in deliverance ministry describe soul ties as deep emotional and spiritual bonds formed through relationships—especially sexual ones—that may remain spiritually significant even after the relationship ends. This concept is extrapolated from passages such as Genesis 2:24 ("the two shall become one flesh") and 1 Samuel 18:1, which describes the close bond between David and Jonathan. The belief is that unhealthy or ungodly soul ties can provide ongoing spiritual influence or oppression.

The concept of "generational curses" or "generational gateways" refers to the idea that patterns of sin or spiritual bondage can be inherited from previous generations. This is based on passages like Exodus 20:5 ("visiting the iniquity of the fathers on the children"), though there is debate among theologians about whether this refers to spiritual inheritance or natural consequences. Some interpret these scriptures as warnings about the social and familial impact of sin, while others see a spiritual dynamic that needs to be addressed through prayer and renunciation.

Trauma and early childhood experiences are also discussed as potential sources of spiritual vulnerability. Some Christian counselors observe that unresolved trauma can have spiritual dimensions, and verses like Psalm 34:18 ("The Lord is close to the brokenhearted") are cited to highlight God's compassion for those who have been wounded. Deliverance ministers may draw from their experience that traumatic events—especially in childhood—can leave individuals open to oppression, though it is important to note that not all Christians understand these connections in the same way.

Unforgiveness and unconfessed sin are frequently cited as significant "legal grounds" for spiritual oppression. Jesus' teaching in Matthew 18:34-35 warns that refusing to forgive others can result in being handed over to "tormentors," which some interpret as a reference to spiritual consequences, while others see it as a figurative warning about psychological or relational harm.

Within the context of spiritual vulnerability and deliverance ministry, three main gateways—personal, generational, and environmental/cultural—are frequently discussed. These gateways represent the various routes through which spiritual influences may gain access, each contributing to layers of potential vulnerability.

- **Personal Gateways (Voluntary Access):** Choices such as persistent sin, unforgiveness, and binding vows are seen as doors we open ourselves. For example, making an inner vow ("I'll never trust again") is thought to create a spiritual tie that can hinder freedom.

- **Generational Gateways (Inherited Access):** Family patterns of sin, addiction, or spiritual oppression are often addressed through prayer and "renunciation of bloodlines," though interpretations vary. Exodus 20:5 and Lamentations 5:7 are frequently cited.

- **Environmental and Cultural Gateways:** Environments saturated with violence, occult practices, or immorality are believed to wear down spiritual resistance. The story of Lot in

Sodom (2 Peter 2:8) is sometimes used to illustrate the impact of a corrupt atmosphere.

It is important to acknowledge that not all Christians or churches agree with every aspect of deliverance ministry or spiritual warfare as described here. Some view these frameworks as helpful guides based on pastoral experience and scriptural interpretation, while others emphasize psychological, relational, or medical factors. A respectful and discerning approach is encouraged, seeking guidance from Scripture, trusted spiritual leaders, and the broader Christian tradition.

The "Two Can't Live Together" Objection

A common pushback says, "If the Holy Spirit lives in me, how could a demon be present too?" The assumption is that salvation instantly fills every part of life. While our theology must be firmly rooted in Scripture, a pastoral approach also requires we listen to the lived experiences of believers who are seeking freedom. Scripture shows that sanctification is progressive:

- The Temple was filled with God's glory, yet later idols were set within its courts.

- The Corinthian church abounded in spiritual gifts while tolerating immorality and division.

- Ananias and Sapphira, members of the Spirit-filled church, yielded to satanic deception.

God does not co-rule with darkness; rather, darkness persists where rooms remain unopened to His cleansing. Demons are not co-owners-they are trespassers on holy ground. Deliverance serves the eviction notice in Jesus' name and closes the door they used to enter.

An Analogy: Deliverance After Salvation

The best analogy for this reality is the process of buying an old house. When you purchase the house, the title and deed are legally transferred-it is fully yours. The old owner has no legal right to it anymore. But that does not mean it is in move-in condition. You may find leftover furniture, faulty wiring, mold in the walls, pests in the attic, and structural damage hidden from plain sight. In the same way, when Christ redeems us, ownership changes instantly. Yet certain "rooms"-habits, memories, vows, soul ties, generational patterns-may still be occupied by remnants of the "old life." These are like old furniture, pests, or even demonic squatters that have no legal right to remain but have not yet been removed. Deliverance is the spiritual 'clean-out and renovation' that follows salvation. The legal ownership has changed, but the house still needs restoring so the new Owner can occupy every room without hindrance.

Biblical and Ministry Precedents

The ministry of Jesus provides a powerful precedent. He did not simply minister to the heathen; He delivered those already familiar with God's covenant. The "daughter of Abraham" in Luke 13:10-16 was bound by a spirit of infirmity for 18 years, yet Jesus did not question her status as a covenant believer. He simply cast out the spirit, freeing her. This shows that deliverance is a normal part of pastoral care for God's people. In the early church, Derek Prince shared compelling accounts of casting out demons from believers who were Spirit-filled, including individuals who held positions of spiritual leadership and responsibility. These testimonies are not isolated;

rather, they reflect a consistent pattern observed in deliverance ministries across the globe. Time and again, committed Christians-people who were baptized in the Holy Spirit, devoted in prayer, and active in their faith communities-found themselves in need of deliverance from demonic oppression. The presence of the Holy Spirit in one's spirit is the very reason deliverance is possible and effective-the stronger power (Luke 11:21-22) drives out the lesser when given full authority.

The Danger of Deliverance Without Discipleship

Jesus warned in Matthew 12:43-45 that if a demon is cast out and the "house" is left empty, the spirit will return with seven worse than itself. This warning applies to believers and unbelievers alike: deliverance must be followed by discipleship, holiness, and continued surrender. Rebecca Brown recounts a tragic case of a young woman named "Chris" who was powerfully delivered but never discipled. Lacking accountability, she returned to bondage in an even worse state. Freedom must be maintained through spiritual growth and vigilance.

Final Thoughts

Demonic oppression does not negate salvation. Christians can be saved, Spirit-filled, and still struggle with spiritual strongholds that require deliverance. Freedom is not automatic; it must be walked out. Deliverance is not about judgment-it's about Jesus' mercy and victory. If you are saved and bound, you do not need to stay that way. Freedom is your inheritance. Let truth, humility, and God's Word guide you into the liberty Christ has secured.

Deliverance After Salvation: Walking in Complete Freedom

1. **Reflect**
   Do you struggle with areas in your life where salvation has not yet brought full freedom-emotionally, mentally, or spiritually?
   Are there habits, thoughts, or reactions that don't align with who you are in Christ, even after you've tried to overcome them?

2. Repent

Acknowledge these areas that may still be under bondage, even as a believer.

Pray: *"Lord, I confess that parts of my life have remained in chains. I surrender them fully to Your sanctifying power."*

3. Respond

Write down one specific area you've rationalized as "just how I am."

Then, declare aloud: *"This part of me is not exempt from Christ's freedom. I renounce every stronghold and receive freedom through Jesus."*

Commit to pursue healing and accountability in that area, actively seeking God's truth and the support of trusted believers.

Chapter 9

CULTS AND THE OCCULT PRACTICES

Satan employs a multitude of snares to ensnare humanity, but few are as dangerous and deceptively attractive as cults and occult practices. These are not harmless alternatives to Christianity or benign curiosities; they are spiritually corrosive systems and direct doorways through which demonic powers gain access, infiltrate lives, and hold people in bondage. As believers called to walk in truth and freedom, we must both understand and expose these works of darkness and be equipped to help others break free.

The Subtle Chains: How Satan Dominates and Deceives

Satan's strategies often express themselves in insidious forms, subtly weaving chains of control and deception around individuals and communities.

When One Person Dominates Another

This control dynamic is especially prominent in **witchcraft**, which can be broadly defined as "the attempt to control another person through spiritual means other than the Holy Spirit." While some manifestations are overt—such as casting spells, curses, or hexes—others are deceptively subtle. These include manipulation through fear, guilt, shame, emotional dependency, or even religious control disguised as piety. Domination bypasses the divine order of freedom in Christ. When someone exerts undue spiritual or emotional influence over another, a demonic foothold can form. Whether through abusive spiritual leaders, manipulative relationships, or deceptive counsel, these actions open doors to tormenting spirits.

The Poison of Heresies and Doctrines of Demons

The spiritual landscape is rife with deceptive teachings. 1 Timothy 4:1 warns: "The Spirit expressly says that in latter times some will depart from the faith, giving heed to deceiving spirits and doctrines of demons." These teachings often contain just enough truth to appear credible but are twisted in subtle, dangerous ways. 2 Peter 2:1 further warns of false teachers who "secretly bring in destructive heresies." These heresies can take many forms: denying the divinity of Christ, rejecting the ultimate authority of Scripture, imposing legalism that leads to spiritual bondage, or promoting hyper-grace doctrines that inadvertently promote sin under the guise of freedom. John wrote of an "antichrist spirit" already present in the world (1 John 4:1-3), actively working to deceive and dilute the pure Gospel.

The Allure of False Religions and Forbidden Paths

Jesus declared in John 14:6, "I am the way, the truth, and the life. No one comes to the Father except through Me." Any spiritual path that denies this singular truth is not simply misinformed—it is spiritually dangerous. False religions offer counterfeit spirituality that, rather than leading to God, invites direct demonic involvement. God strictly prohibits various "forbidden spiritual contacts" (Deuteronomy 18:9-14; Isaiah 47:12-13), including divination, sorcery, interpreting omens, witchcraft, casting spells, consulting mediums and familiar spirits, and necromancy. Engaging in these practices provokes God to judgment and brings spiritual contamination that can affect generations.

Unveiling the Hidden World: Forms and Branches of the Occult

The term "occult" comes from the Latin *occultus*, meaning "hidden" or "secret." It encompasses a vast range of spiritual activities designed to tap into hidden or forbidden knowledge and power, always outside of God's revealed will.

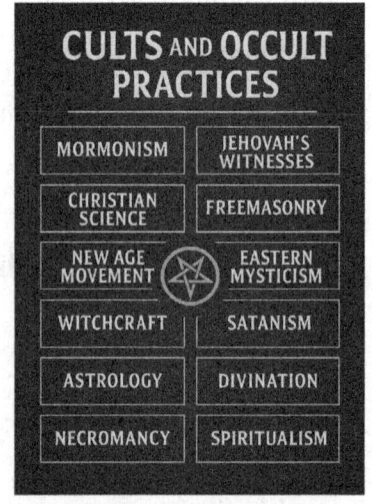

CULTS AND OCCULT PRACTICES

MORMONISM	JEHOVAH'S WITNESSES
CHRISTIAN SCIENCE	FREEMASONRY
NEW AGE MOVEMENT	EASTERN MYSTICISM
WITCHCRAFT	SATANISM
ASTROLOGY	DIVINATION
NECROMANCY	SPIRITUALISM

Seeking Forbidden Knowledge:

The Deception of Divination

Divination is the pursuit of hidden knowledge or guidance through supernatural means apart from God, which is explicitly forbidden in Scripture. While often masked as entertainment or harmless curiosity, these practices serve as spiritual portals through which deceptive spirits gain access, offering counterfeit insight that leads to spiritual bondage and confusion. Common forms include:

- Horoscopes and astrology ("monthly prognosticators" – Isaiah 47:13)
- Tarot cards, pendulums, and crystal balls
- Clairvoyance, psychic readings, and ESP
- Ouija boards and automatic writing
- Necromancy, mediums, and familiar spirits (cf. Deuteronomy 18:10–12)

These practices may seem trivial or entertaining, but they serve as spiritual portals for deceptive spirits to enter, offering counterfeit insight that ultimately leads to bondage.[10]

The Illusion of Control: The Grip of Witchcraft

---

[10] Scripture repeatedly condemns divination and related occult practices as abominations (Deuteronomy 18:10–12; Leviticus 19:31; Acts 16:16–18). These acts invite unclean spirits under the guise of wisdom. See: Prince, Derek. *They Shall Expel Demons*. Chosen Books, 1998, pp. 145–151.

Witchcraft is the direct use of spiritual power to control or manipulate others or circumstances. It is an attempt to bypass God's sovereignty and impose one's will through dark spiritual means. This includes:

- Casting spells, enchantments, and rituals
- Pronouncing curses and hexes
- Practices involving hypnosis and trances Witchcraft appeals to the human desire for control but always brings deeper spiritual enslavement, as it aligns with the kingdom of darkness.

The Subtle Poison: Sorcery and its Modern Guises

The biblical term *pharmakeia* (Galatians 5:20; Revelation 9:21)—from which we derive the modern word "pharmacy"—was used in ancient times to describe sorcery involving the use of potions, drugs, and magical arts. It often included mind-altering substances employed in occult rituals, blending chemical intoxication with spiritual deception.[11] This

---

[11] *Pharmakeia* is translated as "sorcery" or "witchcraft" in many Bible versions. In ancient Greek usage, it referred not only to the practice of

highlights how substances can be used to open spiritual doors. Modern forms of sorcery extend beyond ancient rituals:

- Use of hallucinogens or sedatives to induce altered states in rituals
- Music and dance specifically used to enter trance states for spiritual contact

- Occult-themed games, media, or paraphernalia that normalize or glorify dark spiritual practices Even seemingly innocent forms of entertainment can carry subtle spiritual undertones that foster darkness and spiritual vulnerability.

Other Modern Manifestations of Occult Influence

The occult adapts to contemporary culture, appearing in various forms that may not immediately seem dangerous:

---

magic and spellcasting but also to the use of drugs and potions for occult purposes. See: Strong's Concordance, G5331; Vine, W.E. *Expository Dictionary of New Testament Words*, entry "Sorcery"; Heiser, Michael. *Demons: What the Bible Really Says About the Powers of Darkness*. Lexham Press, 2020, pp. 240–242.

- Eastern meditation practices that aim to empty the mind or connect with spirits apart from Christ.

- Doctrines of reincarnation and karma, which deny the finished work of Christ and the need for salvation.

- Channeling spirits or "spirit guides."

- Yoga practices rooted in Hindu deities or seeking spiritual enlightenment through physical postures, rather than just physical exercise.

- Reiki, energy healing, and various "spiritual cleansing" rituals that draw from non-biblical spiritual sources. These philosophies often mix elements of truth or perceived wellness with subtle spiritual poison, leading individuals away from genuine freedom in Christ.

The Cost of Compromise: Consequences of Occult Involvement

When a person engages in occult practices, even unknowingly, it opens their life to spiritual oppression. These spirits do not remain passive; they actively seek residence and exert influence.

Breaches in the Walls: The Walled City Principle

Proverbs 25:28 says,

> **"Whoever has no rule over his own spirit is like a city broken down, without walls."**

This is the **Walled City Principle**. Our lives are meant to have moral 'walls' of protection which are built by obedience to God's Word and the indwelling Holy Spirit. However, sin  and occult involvement create 'breaches' in these spiritual and moral walls, allowing demonic forces to enter and take control over specific areas of our lives.

Manifestations of Demonic Infiltration: Once access is gained, spirits seek to manifest. Consequences of occult involvement may include:

- Persistent nightmares and night terrors
- Hearing voices or experiencing intrusive, tormenting thoughts
- Unexplained anxiety, panic attacks, or deep depression
- Compulsive behaviors, sexual distortions, or unusual fetishes
- Addiction to substances or destructive patterns
- Chronic torment, confusion, and mental fog These manifestations are often a clear sign that a spiritual entity has gained a foothold.

Securing and Maintaining Freedom: Closing the Doors

Freedom from occult bondage is not a passive process—it demands purposeful, courageous steps and a deep resolve to embrace the light and truth found in Christ. The journey begins with acknowledging the places where darkness has crept in, often through subtle compromise or unaddressed wounds, and recognizing the need for spiritual restoration.

This process calls for genuine self-examination and humility, as it may reveal habits, relationships, or beliefs that have quietly undermined your spiritual defenses. It is important to approach this task with prayerful discernment, seeking the guidance of the Holy Spirit at every stage. True freedom is secured when you commit to repentance, renounce every foothold of the enemy, and intentionally cultivate a life that honors God.

As you confront the remnants of occult influence, remember that each act of confession and renunciation weakens the grip of spiritual oppression and strengthens your inner walls. The path to restoration is marked by persistent faith, spiritual discipline, and a willingness to surrender every area of your life to the authority of Christ. Only then can you walk confidently in the fullness of freedom, guarded by the protective walls built through obedience, prayer, and the active presence of the Holy Spirit.

Renounce and Sever All Contact

Scriptures such as Psalm 139:21-22 reminds us to reject anything opposed to God's will. This includes taking a clear, spoken stand against all involvement with occult practices, objects, and beliefs. Just as in Acts 19:19—where early Christians burned their valuable magic books in public—believers today are urged to take bold, decisive action by:

- **Destroy occult objects:** This includes books, charms, crystals, tarot cards, Ouija boards, idols, symbols, or any item used in occult practices. Physical destruction is a powerful act of severing ties.

- **Cut ties with occult influencers:** This means distancing yourself from unrepentant mediums, psychics, false teachers, or anyone who draws you back into these practices.

- **Renounce aloud all former involvements:** Verbally declare your repentance and renunciation of every specific occult practice or false covenant in Jesus' name.

Repent and Rebuild the Walls

After renouncing, actively ask the Holy Spirit to reveal any remaining breaches in your spiritual walls. Confess these sins, repent of them, and ask for cleansing and forgiveness through Christ's blood. Then, intentionally rebuild your spiritual defenses:

- Immerse yourself in Scripture: Fill your mind with God's truth to counteract the lies of the enemy. As Psalm 119:11 declares, "I have hidden your word in my heart that I might not sin against you."
- Commit to prayer and fasting: Strengthen your spirit and sensitize yourself to the Holy Spirit's leading. Jesus taught in Matthew 26:41, "Watch and pray so that you will not fall into temptation. The spirit is willing, but the flesh is weak."

- Stay accountable to mature believers: Allow trusted spiritual mentors to speak into your life and help you maintain your freedom. Proverbs 27:17 affirms, "As iron sharpens iron, so one person sharpens another."

Fill the House with God's Presence

Matthew 12:43–45 offers a serious warning: when someone is freed from spiritual bondage but does not fill their life with the presence of God, they remain open to even greater attacks. Jesus illustrates this by describing a house swept clean but left empty, making it an easy target for returning darkness. True deliverance isn't just about removing evil influences—it is about inviting God to dwell within. After breaking free, it is crucial to actively pursue God's presence, immerse yourself in His Word, worship, engage in fellowship with other believers, and listen for His guidance through prayer. A life filled with God's light cannot be overtaken by darkness.

- **Be continuously filled with the Holy Spirit:** Cultivate a lifestyle of worship, prayer, and surrender that invites His constant presence.

- **Abide in Christ:** Maintain an intimate, daily relationship with Jesus, drawing your life and strength from Him.

- **Walk in daily obedience and worship:** Let your life be a living sacrifice, honoring God in every thought, word, and deed.

Be continuously filled with the Holy Spirit: Cultivate a lifestyle of worship, prayer, and surrender that invites His constant presence. "Do not get drunk on wine, which leads to debauchery. Instead, be filled with the Spirit." (Ephesians 5:18)

Final Thoughts: Expose and Confront the Darkness

Ephesians 5:11 commands, "And have no fellowship with the unfruitful works of darkness, but rather expose them." As believers, we are not only to avoid occult practices ourselves but to shine the light of Christ into these realms, exposing their deceptive nature. In a culture increasingly fascinated by the supernatural, we must proclaim the truth boldly and without compromise:

- There is no safe form of the occult; all engagement opens doors to darkness.

- False religion is not neutral; it is spiritually toxic and leads away from the one true God.

- Jesus Christ is the only source of true spiritual life, authentic power, and lasting freedom.

With wisdom, discernment, and compassion, we are called to lead others out of the shadows of deception and into the glorious light of God's kingdom. "You shall know the truth, and the truth shall make you free" (John 8:32).

Application Moment: Break Agreement, Break the Chain

1. **Reflect:**
   Have you or your family ever engaged in any occult practices—knowingly or unknowingly? *This could include horoscopes, Ouija boards, mediums, "white magic," or secret religious rituals.*

2. **Repent:**
   "Father, I renounce all involvement in occult or

counterfeit spiritual practices—whether through curiosity, ignorance, or rebellion. Cleanse me by the blood of Jesus. "

3. **Respond:**
Take inventory of your home, books, jewelry, or symbols. Remove and destroy anything linked to occult activity.
Declare aloud:
"I cut every spiritual tie to the occult. Every lingering spirit must leave. I belong to Jesus Christ alone. "

Chapter 10

BREAKING THE CHAINS: STEPS TO PERSONAL DELIVERANCE

Freedom in Christ is not merely a theological concept; it is a lived and transformative reality available to every believer. While Jesus secured our complete liberty through His sacrifice on the cross, walking in that freedom demands intentional, daily engagement. This chapter is designed to be your personal guide—a roadmap for engaging directly with the liberating power of Christ to break spiritual chains. The journey to lasting freedom must address external spiritual oppression, ensuring that the enemy's hold is dismantled.

The First Step: Turning Towards True Freedom Through Repentance

The foundational step in any deliverance process is **repentance**—a sincere and complete turning away from sin and turning toward God. The Greek word *metanoia* implies not just regret or remorse, but a radical transformation of thinking, living, and believing. It's a change of mind that leads to a change in direction, aligning your will with God's.

> **"Repent, and turn to God, so that your sins may be wiped out, that times of refreshing may come from the Lord."**
> **—Acts 3:19**

Jesus always prioritized repentance before healing and deliverance (Mark 1:15). Real repentance is more than an apology; it's a spiritual realignment. It removes the enemy's legal access to your life, dismantling the "legal ground" discussed in Chapter 6, and opens the door to divine intervention. When you genuinely repent, the spiritual ground shifts, and the presence of the Holy Spirit is invited to fill the void once occupied by darkness, bringing times of refreshing and restoration.

Unlocking Your Own Chains: Foundational Steps to Self-Deliverance

While ministry with others is powerful and often necessary for deeper strongholds, there are seasons where God invites you to engage in **self-deliverance**. These moments are deeply personal, and by the Holy

Spirit's help, incredibly effective for addressing various forms of oppression and maintaining your freedom. Speak these declarations aloud, engaging your will and voice in the process, as faith is expressed through confession (Romans 10:10).

Embracing Humility: The Posture of Freedom
Humility is the posture of a dependent heart. It means letting go of self-reliance, pride, and any notion that you can overcome spiritual bondage in your own strength. It's acknowledging your deep need for God's intervention and admitting areas where you've struggled, opened doors, or been influenced. God resists the proud but gives grace to the humble (James 4:10).

- **Declaration:** "Lord, I humble myself before You now. I confess I need Your power and not my own strength. I yield my will fully to Yours, trusting You to set me free."

Shining Light on Secrets: Practice Radical Honesty
Darkness thrives in secrecy. Radical honesty means bringing all sin, shame, and hidden secrets into the purifying light of God's presence (Proverbs 28:13). This

isn't about condemnation, but about allowing God to cleanse. If you have a trusted, mature prayer partner or mentor, confessing to them can bring additional release and accountability (James 5:16).

- **Declaration:** "Holy Spirit, I invite You to search me. Expose any hidden sin, false belief, or unholy soul tie in my life. I choose truth and transparency over secrecy and shame."

Naming the Offense: The Power of Specific Confession General prayers produce general results. Specific confession means naming your sins precisely, without shame, trusting in God's faithfulness to forgive (1 John 1:9). This specificity disarms the enemy, who thrives on vague guilt and accusation.

- **Declaration:** "Father, I confess the sin of [be specific: e.g., anger, lust, pride, idolatry, gossip, controlling behavior, self-pity]. I name it, I acknowledge it as sin against You and others, I repent of it, and I turn from it in Jesus' name. Thank You for forgiving me and cleansing me by the blood of Jesus." (Pause and allow the Holy

Spirit to bring more to mind, confessing each one.)

Breaking All Agreements: Renounce and Sever Ties

Renunciation is a verbal declaration of spiritual divorce from sin, the occult, ungodly beliefs, or any agreements with darkness (whether conscious or unconscious). You are actively turning *away* from these influences and *towards* God. This includes breaking unholy soul ties formed through illicit relationships or controlling bonds.

- **Declaration:** "I now renounce all ties and agreements with [be specific: e.g., horoscopes, the spirit of fear that has plagued me, the lie that I am worthless, any ungodly soul tie with X person, the generational pattern of Y]. I declare that I am dead to this in Christ and alive to God. I break every agreement, covenant, and command all lingering spirits to leave me now in Jesus' name!"

- **Action Step:** If your renunciation involves occult objects (amulets, books, specific jewelry,

119

charms, idols, Ouija boards, etc.), actively destroy or dispose of them. As Acts 19:19 demonstrates, this physical act of severing ties is vital, "lest the spirits have a portal of entry into your home or your life."

Releasing the Captives: The Freedom of Forgiveness

Unforgiveness is a major gateway for demonic torment (Matthew 18:34–35). It's a spiritual stronghold that blocks prayers and gives the enemy a "legal right" to torment you. Forgiveness is a choice of your will, not a feeling. You choose to release the person and the offense to God, relinquishing your right to hold onto bitterness. This also extends to forgiving yourself.

- **Declaration:** "Lord, I choose to forgive [Name of person(s)] for [be specific: e.g., abandoning me, speaking curses over me, rejecting me, abusing me]. I release them from my judgment and give up my right to hold onto this offense. I also forgive myself for [my part in the situation, any self-condemnation, or any ungodly response I had]."

Speaking with Authority: Commanding Deliverance in Jesus' Name

Once sin is confessed and renounced, and forgiveness has been extended, you have legal authority in Christ to expel demonic spirits. This is not a plea, but a command, spoken from your position of authority as a believer (Mark 16:17).

- **Declaration:** "In the mighty name of Jesus Christ, by the power of His shed blood and resurrection, I command every spirit of [e.g., fear, addiction, infirmity, rejection, shame, lust, anger, depression, self-hatred] to go! You have no right here. Leave me now and do not return! I declare myself free in Jesus' name!"

- **Important Note:** For persistent or severe oppression, or if you experience significant manifestations (as discussed in Chapter 12), seeking ministry from a trusted, mature believer or a trained deliverance team is highly recommended. There is wisdom in seeking help when the battle feels overwhelming.

121

Empowering Others: Ministering Deliverance in Community

While personal application of these steps is vital, there is profound power and safety in ministering deliverance within a team context. The early Church operated in community, and Scripture encourages mutual confession and support.

The Power of Team-Based Ministry

Deliverance is safest and most effective when conducted by a team of two or more mature believers (Ecclesiastes 4:9-12). Always have at least two people present, ensuring privacy, integrity, and gender safety (e.g., same-gender ministers for the recipient). This provides spiritual covering and support for both the one ministering and the one receiving.

Creating a Holy Atmosphere

Prior to ministry, prepare the spiritual atmosphere. Begin with heartfelt worship and fervent prayer, inviting the Holy Spirit's presence and leading. Ask the Holy Spirit to reveal any "legal ground" or specific spirits. Fasting, if possible, can further sensitize the ministers to the Holy Spirit's voice and power.

Speaking with Divine Authority: Commanding Demons to Leave

With spiritual discernment (as discussed in Chapter 11) and authority, demons are commanded to leave in Jesus' name. This is not a ritualistic performance but an act of spiritual jurisdiction, based on the authority Christ has given His followers (Mark 16:17). Speak directly and firmly to the demonic spirit, identifying it by name or manifestation if discerned: "Spirit of [name], I command you in Jesus' name—go! You have no right here. Leave now and do not return!"

Sealing the Breakthrough: Essential Aftercare

Immediately following deliverance, it is crucial to ensure the person is filled with the Holy Spirit and guided into practices that maintain their freedom. This "aftercare" is vital to prevent the "empty house" scenario (Matthew 12:43-45).

- Lead them in thanksgiving and worship, solidifying the breakthrough.
- Encourage immediate infilling with the Holy Spirit, inviting His presence to fill any void.

- Assign Scriptures to declare daily, reinforcing truth and identity.
- Urge connection with a local church and an accountability partner (as discussed in Chapter 10).

> **"If the Son sets you free, you will be free indeed." —John 8:36**

Looking Ahead

While breaking spiritual chains is vital, true freedom encompasses the healing of the soul. In **Chapter 11: Healing the Wounded Soul: The Journey of Inner Restoration**, we will explore how past traumas and emotional wounds can be healed by the presence and truth of Jesus Christ, ensuring a holistic path to wholeness.

Application Moment: Embrace the Process

1. **Reflect:**
   Are you ready to apply the steps to freedom, not just in knowledge, but in action and faith?
   What has kept you from fully surrendering to God's healing work—fear, shame, or passivity?

2. **Repent:**
   "God, I repent for resisting the healing process.

I surrender my heart, mind, body, and soul to Your complete work."

3. **Respond:**
   Choose one practical step from the chapter to act on today—such as confession, forgiveness, renunciation, or inviting prayer support.
   Declare aloud:
   "Today, I step into my freedom. What once held me, holds me no longer. I walk in the power of Jesus' name."

Chapter 11

HEALING THE WOUNDED SOUL: THE JOURNEY OF INNER RESTORATION

Deliverance, as explored in Chapter 9A, powerfully breaks spiritual chains, but for freedom to be truly complete and deeply rooted, inner healing mends the soul. Many spiritual strongholds are rooted not just in sin, but in unhealed trauma, deep betrayal, or identity wounding that occurred early in life. These soul wounds provide fertile ground for demonic influence, and without addressing them, a person may experience re-entry of spirits or repeat cycles of bondage. This chapter will guide you through the profound journey of emotional healing, where the presence and truth of Jesus Christ bring restoration to the deepest parts of your being.

> "He heals the brokenhearted and binds up their wounds." —Psalm 147:3

Emotional healing is the binding, restoring, and sealing of the heart, bringing wholeness to the inner person. It addresses the pain of the past so that the enemy has no foothold in the present, allowing you to walk in the fullness of the abundant life Christ promised.

Unveiling the Wounds: Key Areas of Emotional Pain

Our emotional landscape can be deeply scarred by life's experiences, creating vulnerabilities that the enemy can exploit. Recognizing these key areas of emotional wounding is the first step towards healing:

- **Abandonment:** This wound often results in a deep fear of intimacy, self-rejection, a constant need for external validation, or a struggle to trust others.
- **Abuse (Verbal, Sexual, Emotional):** These traumatic experiences leave deep scars of shame, confusion, fragmentation of identity, and profound difficulty trusting others or even oneself.
- **Fear & Anxiety:** While sometimes demonic, these pervasive emotions are often deeply rooted

in unhealed trauma, a persistent sense of insecurity, or past experiences of terror.

- **Rejection & Shame:** These painful experiences can create lifelong emotional patterns that attract spiritual oppression, leading to isolation, people-pleasing behaviors, or self-sabotage.

- **Betrayal:** This wound results in guardedness, bitterness, difficulty trusting others, and a hardened heart, often leading to a reluctance to form new, healthy relationships.

Encountering the Great Physician: Techniques for Inner Healing

Healing flows from the active presence of God and the intentional application of His Word to our wounded places. Scripture declares, "He sent His word and healed them" (Psalm 107:20), revealing that healing is not just emotional but deeply spiritual. Jesus, the Great Physician (Luke 5:31), came to "heal the brokenhearted" and set the captives free (Isaiah 61:1; Luke 4:18). True restoration occurs when we invite His presence into our pain and align our thinking with His truth. As we do, lies are dismantled, strongholds are broken, and freedom is secured—for it is the truth that makes us free (John 8:32).

Inviting Jesus into Your Pain: Guided Prayer & Visualization

The following sacred practice creates space for Jesus to minister directly into your wounded places. Through prayerful visualization, you welcome the Great Physician into your memories—not to erase the past, but to redeem it with His truth, presence, and healing love.

Step 1: Prepare the Atmosphere

Find a quiet, undisturbed space. Close your eyes and take a few deep breaths. Invite the Holy Spirit to be present with you, as Jesus promised:

> *"The Helper, the Holy Spirit… will teach you all things…"* **(John 14:26, NKJV).**

Ask Him to bring to your mind a specific painful memory, recurring negative emotion, or unhealed wound that needs His touch.

Step 2: Visualize Jesus in the Memory

As the memory or emotion arises, allow yourself to feel the reality of that moment. Now, invite Jesus into that scene—just as it was. Don't try to change the memory; simply invite Him into it.

- What is Jesus doing?
- What is He saying?
- How is He responding to the people or the situation?

If you recall a moment of **rejection**, see Him embrace you and whisper, *"You are accepted in the Beloved" (Ephesians 1:6).* If the memory involves **fear**, visualize Him standing beside you, radiating calm, declaring:

> *"Peace I leave with you, My peace I give to you..." (John 14:27).*

Let His presence rewrite the emotional narrative and replace the lie that took root.

Step 3: Release the Pain

Allow yourself to feel any sadness, fear, grief, or anger—right there in Jesus' presence. Don't suppress the emotions. Instead, surrender them.

> **"Casting all your care upon Him, for He cares for you." (1 Peter 5:7, NKJV).**

Picture yourself handing Him the burden. You may see Him taking it, absorbing it, or even destroying it. Let the pain dissolve in His love. He is not repelled by your wounds—He died to heal them.

Testimony: When Jesus Sat in the Car with Me

For years, I carried a deep well of **unforgiveness** toward someone who had wounded me. I wouldn't have admitted it out loud, but the bitterness festered beneath the surface. Almost every night, I had the same disturbing dream: I was behind the wheel of a car, and I kept hitting the person—again and again. It felt like a cycle I couldn't escape. I woke up angry and ashamed.

Then one night, the dream shifted. As I was gripping the wheel, ready to strike again, I glanced to the passenger seat—and there sat **Jesus**.

He didn't raise His voice. He didn't condemn me. He just looked at me with deep, piercing eyes and asked, *"How long are we going to keep doing this?"*

That single question broke something open in me. I

wept in the dream—and when I woke up, the rage was gone. I never had that dream again.

Jesus didn't lecture me. He simply sat with me in my pain, spoke the truth in love, and invited me to choose healing.

Transforming Your Thoughts: Renewing the Mind

Unhealed wounds often create corresponding lies that you believe about yourself, others, or God (e.g., "I'm not good enough," "I'm unlovable," "I'll always be alone," "God can't be trusted"). Renewing your mind means actively identifying these lies and replacing them with God's unchanging truth (Romans 12:2).

- **Identify the Lie:** Pinpoint the specific lie associated with the wound.

- **Replace with Truth:** Memorize and declare your identity in Christ daily.
  Example: If the lie is "I'm unlovable," declare: "I am loved with an everlasting love (Jeremiah 31:3). I am fearfully and wonderfully made

(Psalm 139:14). Christ demonstrates His own love toward me in that while I was still a sinner, Christ died for me (Romans 5:8)."

- **Journaling for Breakthrough:** Dedicate a journal to this process. For each identified lie, write it down. Then, write the corresponding truth from Scripture. Finally, write a daily declaration based on that truth and speak it aloud. This consistent practice solidifies the new truth in your mind and spirit.

Honoring Your Pain: The Role of Lament & Healthy Grief

Unresolved emotional wounds often stem from unacknowledged losses—loss of innocence, trust, safety, connection, or even a perceived future. Healthy grieving, or lament, is the process of acknowledging these losses and expressing the associated pain to God. It's not self-pity, but a raw, honest outpouring of your heart to a compassionate Father (Psalm 34:18).

- **Give Voice to Your Pain:** Use prayer, journaling, or even crying out to God to express your sorrow, anger, confusion, and disappointment. Don't censor yourself; God can handle your raw emotions (Psalm 62:8).

- **Utilize Psalms of Lament:** Read and pray through psalms of lament (e.g., Psalm 13, Psalm 22, Psalm 60, Psalm 88). These psalms provide a divine template for expressing deep pain while still acknowledging God's presence and character.

- **Process, Don't Suppress:** Suppressing emotions can create a breeding ground for spiritual and emotional issues, allowing bitterness or resentment to take root (Ephesians 4:26-27). Healthy lament allows these emotions to be processed in a safe, godly way, leading to release, healing, and eventual peace.

Building New Foundations: Establishing New Emotional Habits

True healing doesn't end with the removal of pain—it continues with the **construction of new emotional pathways** that align with God's truth. Emotional healing is not simply the absence of torment, but the presence of Christ-formed responses that shape your character and restore your soul.

Rather than being trapped by destructive reactions, it's essential to nurture **godly emotional habits** rooted in love, truth, and identity in Christ. This transformation is not instantaneous. It is cultivated through **intentional practice**, Spirit-led awareness, and a willingness to surrender old patterns to God's renewing power (Romans 12:2).

Be patient with yourself during this journey. Healing often requires revisiting past wounds, confronting inner narratives, and choosing healthier responses in real time. Over time, what once triggered fear, anger, or despair will become an opportunity to **respond with peace, confidence, and grace**. This is the evidence of emotional maturity in Christ and the fruit of Spirit-led sanctification.

Practical Tools to Build New Emotional Habits

- **Respond vs. React**

  Learn to pause before reacting emotionally. When a trigger arises, ask: *"Is this response flowing from truth and trust—or from past wounds and fear?"* This moment of pause invites the Holy Spirit to guide your emotions and anchor your heart (cf. Proverbs 4:23).

- **Identify Triggers & Pre-Plan Your Response**

  Become aware of specific people, phrases, or situations that stir emotional unrest. Then **intentionally craft a godly response**. *Example:* If criticism causes shame, counter it with affirmations of your identity in Christ (Ephesians 1:6). Instead of withdrawing, consider asking, *"Can you clarify what you meant?"* to remain grounded in peace.

- **Practice Daily Gratitude**

  Develop a habit of giving thanks throughout the day. Gratitude realigns your focus from lack to abundance, from pain to God's provision.

> "In everything give thanks..." (1 Thessalonians 5:18).

Start and end your day listing 3–5 things you're truly thankful for—it retrains your emotions to expect goodness.

- **Cultivate Compassion—For Yourself and Others**

  Dismantle harsh self-judgment and replace it with kindness. Extend the same grace to others that Christ extended to you.

  > *"Put on... compassion, kindness, humility..."* (Colossians 3:12).

  Speak to yourself with tenderness, recognizing that emotional growth is a process, not a performance.

- **Practice Christ-Centered Mindfulness**

  Be present. Ground yourself in the awareness of Christ's nearness rather than dwelling on past hurts or future anxieties.

  > **"Be *anxious* for nothing[...] and the peace of God[...]will guard your hearts**

and minds[...]" (Philippians 4:6–7).

Whisper simple truths throughout your day like: *"Jesus, You are here." "I am safe in Your love."*

Soaking in the Father's Love: The Ultimate Healing Balm Many inner wounds trace back to a distorted or absent view of the Father's love. Healing often requires a deep revelation of God's perfect, unconditional love (1 John 4:18). The experience of the Father's affection silences shame, uproots rejection, and brings a profound sense of security and belonging.

- **Practice:** Spend time meditating on Scriptures about God's love (e.g., Romans 8:38-39, Zephaniah 3:17). Ask the Holy Spirit to pour out the Father's love into your heart (Romans 5:5). This transformative love reinforces deliverance by sealing the soul with peace, identity, and renewed trust in God, making it easier to maintain freedom.

Looking Ahead With the chains of personal oppression broken and the wounds of the soul restored, you are now equipped for a life of sustained freedom. In **Chapter 10:**

Be Intentional – Getting and Maintaining Your Deliverance, we will explore the essential disciplines and mindset needed to steward your freedom and walk in continuous victory, ensuring your spiritual house remains filled and guarded.

Application Moment: Invite God Into the Wounds

1. **Reflect:**
    What past wound—rejection, betrayal, abuse, loss—still affects how you see yourself or others today?
    Have you tried to ignore the pain rather than invite God into it?

2. **Repent:**
    "Lord, I've held on to pain instead of surrendering it to You. Forgive me for protecting my wounds instead of letting You heal them."

3. **Respond:**
    Write a letter to God expressing the wound. Then pray:
    "I release this hurt into Your hands. I invite You, Jesus, into every place I've hidden. Restore my soul."

Chapter 12

BE INTENTIONAL – GETTING AND MAINTAINING YOUR DELIVERANCE

The air in Sarah's small apartment felt different. Lighter. For weeks, a suffocating heaviness had clung to her, a spirit of anxiety that had stolen her sleep and choked her joy. But after a powerful session of prayer and deliverance, a tangible peace had settled. She felt unburdened, as if a great weight had been lifted from her shoulders. She breathed deeply, a true, unhindered breath for the first time in months. *This is it,* she thought, *I'm finally free.*

Yet, a few weeks later, a subtle unease began to creep back. First, a familiar thought, a whisper of worry. Then, a restless night. Soon, the old anxieties, though not as crushing, began to circle like vultures, testing the boundaries of her newfound peace. Sarah realized that while the breakthrough was real, the battle for sustained freedom had just begun. Deliverance, she discovered, was not the final destination; it was a powerful, divine doorway into a new quality of life. The moment of freedom, whether from demonic torment, emotional bondage, or generational patterns, marks a profound beginning. However, staying free requires **intentional, Spirit-led living.** Just like a house that has been swept clean, your life must be actively filled with the presence of God and guarded with spiritual vigilance to prevent darkness from returning. This chapter will equip you with the essential disciplines and mindset needed to steward your freedom and walk in sustained victory.

The Peril of the Empty House: Why Freedom Demands Vigilance

Sarah's experience mirrors a sobering warning Jesus gave in Matthew 12:43–45. He spoke of an unclean spirit leaving a person, only to wander through dry places, seeking rest. If it returns to find its former home "empty, swept, and put in order," it brings with it seven more spirits more wicked than itself, and the last state of that person is worse than the first.

The implication is chillingly clear: **neutrality is**

dangerous. A spiritual void, even one created by a powerful deliverance, is an invitation for greater darkness. Deliverance without ongoing discipleship, infilling, and active maintenance is a setup for relapse. Freedom is not a one-time event that guarantees perpetual liberty without further effort. It is like a garden—it must be **tended daily**. What you feed, grows. What you ignore, decays. Your spiritual "house" must be intentionally occupied and guarded, not left vacant for the enemy to re-inhabit.

Building Your Fortress: Seven Pillars of a Delivered Life

For Sarah, and for you, maintaining deliverance and walking in consistent victory isn't about striving in your own strength, but about embracing spiritual disciplines. These are not optional accessories; they are essential practices that fortify your spiritual "house" and establish an environment where the Holy Spirit thrives, making it an unwelcome place for darkness.

1. **Enthroning Christ: Lordship Over Every Domain** This is the bedrock upon which all lasting

freedom is built (Romans 12:1–2). Imagine your life as a kingdom, and Jesus as the King. You are urged to offer every part of yourself—your mind, body, emotions, will, finances, relationships, career, and future—as a living sacrifice to Him. Any area you withhold, any secret compartment you keep locked away from Christ's Lordship, can become a foothold or a re-entry point for the enemy. It's where the "old tenant" might try to slip back in. Regularly invite the Holy Spirit to shine His light into any unyielded areas. Consciously surrender them to Jesus. This might involve changing a stubborn habit, extending forgiveness to someone you've resisted, or letting go of control in a specific situation. Daily, declare, "Jesus, You are Lord over [name specific area of your life, e.g., my finances, my thought life, my relationships]."

2. **Living Saturated: The Spirit's Constant Infilling**
Paul's command, "Be filled with the Spirit," is an ongoing imperative, not a one-time event from your conversion (Ephesians 5:18). It means to be continually replenished, controlled, and empowered by the Holy Spirit. This divine infilling displaces

darkness, fills the "swept house" with God's radiant presence, and leaves no room for the enemy. Cultivate a lifestyle that actively invites the Spirit's presence. This includes heartfelt worship, consistent and fervent prayer (including praying in the Spirit/tongues), regularly yielding your will and desires to God's, and promptly obeying the Spirit's gentle leading in your daily life.

3. **The Unshakeable Foundation: Living by God's Word** The Word of God is more than just a book; it is a living, active force (Psalm 119:11). It serves as both a mirror (revealing truth about yourself and God) and a powerful weapon against the enemy's lies (Matthew 4:4). It renews your mind, exposes deception, and equips you for every good work, making your spiritual house strong and filled with light. Commit to consistent daily reading, memorize key verses to resist temptation, ponder and chew on Scripture through meditation, and actively apply biblical principles to your daily life and decisions.

When tempted, speak the Word aloud, just as Jesus did when confronted by Satan in the wilderness.

4. **Clothed in Christ: Put on Your Spiritual Armor** Freedom requires constant protection. Paul describes spiritual armor, not as optional accessories for special occasions, but as essential pieces for daily spiritual warfare (Ephesians 6:10–18). This armor is Christ Himself, and we "put it on" by actively embracing and living out the truths it represents, making us impervious to the enemy's attacks. Begin each day by consciously "donning" each piece, visualizing yourself putting on God's protection: the Belt of Truth, Breastplate of Righteousness, Shoes of the Gospel of Peace, Shield of Faith, Helmet of Salvation, and the Sword of the Spirit (the Word of God). Maintain constant, Spirit-led communication with God through prayer, empowering all other pieces of armor.

5. **Strength in Unity: The Power of Godly Community** Isolation is a dangerous trap for the enemy. He thrives in darkness and solitude. Fellowship with other Spirit-filled believers strengthens your faith, provides encouragement, and

keeps you accountable (Hebrews 10:25; 1 John 1:7). You need a community that can speak truth into your life, pray with you, and stand with you in times of spiritual attack. Be an active and committed part of a local, Bible-believing church. Join a small group or find a trusted mentor for deeper connection and accountability. Consciously distance yourself from environments or relationships that tempt you back into bondage, drain your spiritual energy, or undermine your spiritual growth.

6. **Humble Strength: Embracing Spiritual Covering Against Rebellion**, even subtle forms of it, weakens your spiritual defenses and opens doors to pride. Humbly honoring the pastors, mentors, or leaders God places in your life provides a layer of spiritual protection, wisdom, and covering (Hebrews 13:17; 1 Peter 5:5–8). Seek counsel from trusted spiritual leaders when facing significant decisions or struggles. Be open to gentle correction and instruction from those God has placed over you. Actively support your spiritual authorities in prayer. Recognize that submission is not blind obedience;

it's a humble posture within healthy, biblical boundaries that promote growth and freedom.

7. **The Central Anchor: Keeping Jesus at the Core**
Jesus is not just Savior—He is Lord, the very center and sustainer of all things (Colossians 1:17). He is the one who holds all things together. Keep Him central in every decision, every ambition, every relationship, and every aspect of your daily life. Where Jesus truly rules, darkness cannot linger. He is the light that dispels all shadows. Prioritize dedicated time with Jesus each day, making Him your first love. Involve Him in your plans and choices, seeking His will above your own. Let your passionate love for Him be the driving force behind all you do.

Daily Rhythms of Liberty: Cultivating Sustained Freedom

Beyond these seven foundational pillars, cultivating specific daily habits will reinforce your freedom, making it a natural and effortless part of your life. These are the small, consistent actions that build spiritual muscle and keep your "house" vibrant and occupied.

Constant Communion: The Breath of Daily Prayer
Prayer is your constant lifeline to the Source of all strength (Matthew 6:6; Ephesians 6:18). Don't limit it to formal times or specific requests. Practice conversational prayer throughout your day, talking to God about everything. Include different types of prayer: heartfelt praise and thanksgiving, fervent intercession for others, authoritative spiritual warfare prayers (commanding the enemy), and quiet listening prayer for divine guidance.

Keeping Short Accounts: The Cleansing of Quick Confession Don't allow unconfessed sin to accumulate like spiritual dust. Keep "short accounts" with God and others (1 John 1:9). As soon as you recognize sin in your thoughts, words, or actions, confess it immediately. This swift action prevents the enemy from gaining a foothold through guilt, shame, or unrighteousness.

The Shield of Love: Walking in Forgiveness and Grace Actively choose to love, even when it's difficult or when you feel hurt. Resist bitterness, offense, and strife (Romans 12:21). Forgiveness is not a one-time event but an ongoing practice. Love is a powerful spiritual shield that extinguishes the enemy's attempts to create division, hurt, and open doors for bitterness (1 John 4:7-8).

Sharpening Your Spirit: Engaging Key Disciplines Cultivate specific spiritual disciplines regularly to strengthen your inner person. Periodically abstain from food or other things through **fasting** to sharpen your spiritual senses, humble yourself, and break the power of the flesh over your life. Keep a spiritual **journal** to record your prayers, insights from Scripture, and experiences with God. This helps you process emotions, track your spiritual growth, and remember God's faithfulness. Engage in personal **worship** through song, dance, or simply adoring God in your heart. Let worship be a constant atmosphere in your life. **Commit key verses to memory**—especially those related to your identity in Christ, God's power, and spiritual warfare. These become ready weapons in times of temptation.

A Public Declaration: The Significance of Baptism If you haven't been water baptized since your conversion, prayerfully consider it. It's a powerful, biblical act that publicly symbolizes your death to sin and your old life, and your resurrection with Christ into new life (Romans 6:4; 1 Corinthians 10:1–2). It can be a significant spiritual point of cutting ties with the enemy's past claims over your life.

Standing Guard: Recognizing and Resisting the Enemy's Return

Sarah learned that the enemy is persistent. After a breakthrough, he may attempt to return, often subtly, by tempting you with old thought patterns, emotional triggers, or familiar temptations. This is not a sign of failure, but a test of your resolve.

Recognizing Warning Signs: Be acutely alert to:

- **Old thought loops:** Negative, condemning, or obsessive thoughts you thought were gone, trying to re-establish themselves.

- **Familiar emotional patterns:** Sudden surges of fear, anger, depression, or shame without an obvious external cause, indicating an internal spiritual nudge.

- **Renewed temptations:** Strong, persistent urges towards past sins or destructive habits you believed were broken.

- **Spiritual lethargy:** A sudden, unexplained loss of desire for prayer, reading the Word, or engaging in fellowship.

Resist Immediately:

- **Immediate Confrontation:** As soon as you recognize an attack, immediately confront it with the Word of God and the authority of Jesus' name. Speak aloud, "Get behind me, Satan!" (Matthew 16:23). Do not entertain the thought or feeling.

- **Fill the Void:** Replace every negative thought or temptation with a corresponding truth from Scripture. If the enemy whispers a lie, declare God's truth aloud. For example, if he whispers "You're worthless," declare, "I am fearfully and wonderfully made, and God's thoughts toward me are precious" (Psalm 139:14, 17).

- **Re-engage Disciplines:** If you feel a spiritual lull or a subtle return, intentionally ramp up your prayer, worship, and Scripture intake. These are your spiritual immune boosters.

Stay Spiritually Aware:

Cultivating Discernment for Maintenance

- **Listen to the Holy Spirit:** Pay attention to the "still, small voice" (1 Kings 19:12) that warns you, prompts you, or brings a sense of unease.

- **Test the Spirits:** (1 John 4:1) Learn to discern if a thought, suggestion, or feeling is from God, your own flesh, or the enemy. Ask: "Does this align with Scripture? Does it bring peace or confusion? Does it glorify God?"

- **Seek Confirmation:** If you are unsure about a spiritual impression or persistent struggle, discuss it with a trusted spiritual mentor or accountability partner. Do not try to figure it out alone.

Not Alone: The Unbreakable Cord of Accountability

While self-deliverance and personal disciplines are vital, God designed us for community. Accountability is a powerful tool for maintaining freedom, providing a safety net and a source of strength.

Why Accountability is Crucial:

- **Shared Burden:** "Bear one another's burdens, and so fulfill the law of Christ" (Galatians 6:2). You don't have to carry it all alone.

- **Protection:** A threefold cord is not easily broken (Ecclesiastes 4:12). An accountability partner or group provides a spiritual covering and a defense against isolation, which is the enemy's favorite tactic.

- **Blind Spots:** Others can often see things in our lives—patterns, temptations, unyielded areas— that we cannot see ourselves.

- **Encouragement:** They can cheer you on, remind you of truth when you forget, and pray with you through difficult times.

Finding Godly Accountability:

- **Choose Wisely:** Select someone mature in faith, trustworthy, discreet, and deeply committed to biblical principles. This is a sacred trust.

- **Be Specific:** Agree on what you will be accountable for (e.g., daily disciplines, specific temptations, emotional responses, areas of weakness). Ambiguity breeds failure.

- **Regular Check-ins:** Establish a consistent schedule for connecting (weekly, bi-weekly, or as needed) to share honestly and pray together.

What Accountability Looks Like:

- **Honest Sharing:** Openly share your struggles, temptations, and victories, even when it's uncomfortable.

- **Mutual Encouragement:** Affirm and build each other up in faith, reminding each other of God's promises and power.

- **Gentle Correction:** Be willing to receive and offer loving, biblical correction when needed, always in humility and grace.

- **Consistent Prayer:** Pray specifically and
  fervently for each other's freedom and growth.

> **"Resist the devil, and he will flee from
> you." —James 4:7**

Deliverance is both a moment and a journey. The miracle may happen in an instant, but maintenance is lifelong. Resistance requires both **submission to God** and **proactive effort**. It's not about earning your freedom—it's about stewarding it. By embracing these pillars and daily practices, and by walking in the strength of godly community, you can walk in sustained liberty and become a powerful testament to Christ's delivering power.

Sustaining Your Freedom: What Comes Next?

Now that you've been equipped with the tools to walk in freedom and maintain it daily, the next step is to sharpen your spiritual senses. In the next chapter, we will explore the crucial role of **discernment**—how to identify the true source of a problem and recognize the Holy Spirit's leading for effective deliverance.

Application Moment: Make Freedom a Lifestyle

1. **Reflect:**
   Have you treated deliverance as a one-time event instead of a lifestyle?
   What choices do you need to make daily to walk in sustained freedom?

2. **Repent:**
   "God, forgive me for being passive with my freedom. Help me to be intentional and disciplined in my walk with You."

3. **Respond:**
   Choose one area—daily prayer, Scripture, fasting, or community support—to recommit to as a guardrail for freedom.
   Say aloud:
   "I will not return to bondage. I will walk intentionally in the freedom Christ has given me."

Chapter 13

DISCERNMENT – A KEY TO EFFECTIVE DELIVERANCE

In the realm of spiritual warfare and deliverance, the ability to discern is not merely a helpful skill—it is an indispensable spiritual gift and a cultivated discipline. Imagine navigating a dense fog without a compass, or trying to identify an enemy in camouflage. Without discernment, even the most well-intentioned efforts can be misdirected, ineffective, or even harmful. This chapter will define biblical discernment, explain its critical importance in deliverance ministry, explore its various facets, provide practical steps for cultivating it, and highlight common pitfalls to avoid, ensuring your spiritual vision is clear and sharp.

Seeing Beyond the Surface: The Essence of Spiritual Discernment

Spiritual discernment is the God-given ability to perceive what is not immediately obvious to the natural senses. It's a divine intuition, enabling believers to distinguish between good and evil, truth and deception, the divine and the demonic, and the subtle influences of the flesh versus the leading of the Spirit. It is a spiritual sense, allowing believers to "test the spirits" (1 John 4:1) and understand the unseen realities at play in any given situation.

In the context of deliverance, discernment is crucial because demonic activity often masquerades, hides, or blends seamlessly with natural human struggles. Without this spiritual insight, we might:

- **Misattribute Natural Problems:** We might mistakenly blame a demon for a problem that has natural or psychological roots, leading to unnecessary or misdirected deliverance efforts.

- **Overlook Demonic Issues:** Conversely, we could overlook genuine demonic influence by simply blaming natural causes, inadvertently leaving a person in spiritual bondage.

- **Misidentify the Enemy:** We might misunderstand a demonic spirit's specific nature or assignment, resulting in ineffective ministry because we're not addressing the true source.

- **Miss God's Leading:** Crucially, a lack of discernment can cause us to miss the Holy Spirit's precise timing, specific instructions, or gentle leading, hindering the entire deliverance process.

The Holy Spirit's Lens: Different Facets of Discernment

Discernment is multifaceted, operating in various ways to provide clarity and precision for effective ministry, much like different lenses on a camera reveal different details.

Discerning Spirits: Unmasking the Unseen (1 Corinthians 12:10) This is a specific spiritual gift that enables a believer to perceive the presence, nature, and source of a spirit—whether it is the Holy Spirit at work, a human spirit (e.g., a person's own thoughts or emotions), or an evil spirit.

- **In Deliverance:** This gift is invaluable. It allows the minister to identify if a problem is indeed demonic, and if so, what kind of spirit it might be (e.g., a spirit of fear, a spirit of infirmity, a lying spirit). It helps differentiate between a person's personality or fleshly reactions and the distinct influence of a demon.

- **Manifestations of Discernment:** This discernment may come as a sudden "knowing" in your spirit, a strong impression, a word of knowledge, a physical sensation (e.g., heaviness, coldness, nausea in the minister's own body), or even a brief visual or mental impression (like seeing an image of the spirit's influence).

Discerning the Source: Unraveling the Roots of a Problem

> "Not every storm is demonic—but every storm needs discernment."

In deliverance ministry, it is vital to exercise Spirit-led discernment before labeling every issue as demonic. The Apostle Paul teaches in 1 Thessalonians 5:21, "Test all things; hold fast what is good." Similarly, Hebrews 5:14 commends spiritual maturity as the ability "to discern both good and evil." This principle is essential when ministering to those who are emotionally wounded, spiritually oppressed, or psychologically burdened.

Consider Jesus' approach: in Mark 9:25, He rebukes a deaf and mute spirit directly—but in John 5, He heals a lame man without mention of demons. Jesus never used a one-size-fits-all model. Instead, He exemplified wisdom in distinguishing between physical illness, sin, trauma, and demonic presence.

A woman, we will call her Angela, came for help after years of anxiety and depression. Some believed she simply needed medication. Others declared it was a "spirit of fear." But deeper prayer and counsel revealed both were true: childhood trauma had wounded her soul, creating an opening for demonic torment. Her deliverance required pastoral care, healing prayer, and renewed thinking. Discernment, not assumption, brought her into freedom.

Six Possible Roots Beneath the Surface

1. Sometimes It's Demonic

The Bible is clear that demons are real spiritual

beings who can torment individuals, influence behaviors, and even afflict the body. Jesus cast out demons frequently (e.g., Mark 1:34, Luke 8:2). A man tormented by a legion of demons in *Mark 5* was isolated, self-harming, and overtaken by dark forces. His deliverance came only when Jesus commanded the spirits to leave.

But demonic oppression is not always so visible. It may appear as persistent torment, unexplainable fear, or resistance to spiritual things. *Luke 13:11* tells of a woman "bound by a spirit of infirmity for eighteen years." She was in the synagogue—faithful, but afflicted.

Discernment is key. When spiritual authority is needed, counseling won't suffice. But if the issue is not spiritual, casting out demons may cause confusion or spiritual harm.

2. Sometimes It's the Flesh

The Bible teaches that our carnal nature—what Paul calls "the flesh"—can produce sinful behaviors without demonic assistance. *Galatians 5:19–21* lists the works of the flesh: "hatred, jealousy, outbursts of wrath, selfish ambitions, dissensions..." These are learned patterns and uncrucified desires—not necessarily demonic activity.

A man who constantly lashes out in anger may blame a "spirit of rage," when what he truly needs is repentance, accountability, and Spirit-led self-control (*Galatians 5:22–23*). As *James 1:14–15* warns, "Each one is tempted when he is drawn away by his own desires and enticed."

Some habits are not strongholds. They are just undisciplined flesh that needs crucifying.

3. Sometimes It's Psychological or Natural

God designed us as integrated beings—spirit, soul, and body (*1 Thessalonians 5:23*). Mental illness, trauma, or medical conditions are very real and often misunderstood in spiritual circles.

> **Proverbs 18:13 warns, "He who answers a matter before he hears it, it is folly and shame to him."**

We must not assume every emotional or physical affliction is spiritual.

163

A *young* woman with bipolar disorder may need medication and trauma therapy in addition to prayer. A man with PTSD from childhood abuse may need inner healing and deliverance—but also safety, counseling, and time.

Jesus *healed* the body, soul, and spirit—He never ignored one for the other (*Matthew 4:24*).

4. **Often, It's a Mixture**

Most commonly, people experience a combination of emotional wounds, sinful behaviors, and spiritual oppression. For instance, *Ephesians 4:26–27* warns, "Be angry and do not sin... nor give place to the devil." This suggests unresolved emotional issues (like anger) can become spiritual doorways when not dealt with.

A person may struggle with anxiety due to childhood trauma (emotional), which leads to coping through sin (flesh), and opens the door to fear or torment (demonic). Only wise, Spirit-led counsel can properly discern these intertwined layers and minister freedom in all dimensions.

5. Sometimes It's Human Error

Some problems are not demonic, emotional, or psychological—they are the result of poor choices or ignorance. Scripture constantly calls God's people to pursue wisdom:

> **"The simple believes every word, but the prudent considers well his steps." (Proverbs 14:15)**

> *"There is a way that seems right to a man, but its end is the way of death." (Proverbs 14:12)*

Many believers suffer not because of demonic attack, but because they acted without counsel, ignored wisdom, or repeated cycles of dysfunction. A person who ignores budgeting principles and ends up in debt may blame the "spirit of poverty," but the real issue is poor financial stewardship. A failed relationship might not be the devil—it could be the fruit of ignoring godly boundaries or rushing into things.

God is merciful, but He doesn't override free will. When human error is the source, the solution is humility, repentance, learning, and obedience. You don't need deliverance from what you need to learn from.

6. **Sometimes** It's the Brokenness of the Times

We are living in what Scripture calls *"perilous times." (2 Timothy 3:1–5)* Paul describes a generation marked by pride, rebellion, and a form of godliness without power.

Jesus also warned in *Matthew 24:12, "Because lawlessness will abound, the love of many will grow cold."* The days we live in are filled with stress, anxiety, cultural confusion, and spiritual warfare in the atmosphere. Many believers are weighed down by this ambient pressure—not because of personal sin, but because of the condition of the world.

Consider Daniel. He fasted and mourned, not just for his own sin, but for the sins of his nation (*Daniel 9*). Similarly, Lot was *"tormented in his righteous soul by the lawless deeds he saw and heard"* (*2 Peter 2:8*).

Sometimes your heaviness isn't internal—it's the grief of a godly soul in a wicked culture.

In these cases, the call isn't necessarily to cast out a demon but to anchor deeper in God's presence, truth, and community. Jesus didn't pray for the Father to remove us from the world, but to protect us in it (*John 17:15*).

Discernment means asking: What's the source? What's the wound? What's the pattern? What's the stronghold?

Discerning God's Blueprint: Timing and Method

Discernment also guides the practical application of ministry, ensuring we align with God's perfect plan:

- **Divine Timing:** Discernment helps know *when* to minister deliverance. Is the person truly ready to receive? Have they completed the necessary steps of repentance and forgiveness? Is the environment spiritually safe and conducive for ministry?

- **God's Method:** It guides *how* to minister. Does the situation require a gentle, quiet prayer, or a strong, authoritative command? Is inner healing needed first before deliverance? Is there a specific "legal ground" (as discussed in Chapter 5) that must be addressed before the spirit will leave?

Sharpening Your Spiritual Senses: Cultivating Discernment

Discernment is both a divine gift freely given by the Holy Spirit and a skill that must be developed through intentional practice and humble submission to God.

Deepening Intimacy with the Holy Spirit

The Holy Spirit is the Spirit of Truth and our ultimate Helper in discernment. The more intimately you know His voice and presence, the easier it is to recognize what is *not* Him.

- **Cultivate Intimacy:** Spend consistent, quality time in prayer, heartfelt worship, and quiet listening in His presence.

- **Embrace Yieldedness:** Be fully yielded to His voice and leading. Discernment flows most freely from a surrendered heart.

Anchoring in Truth: Immerse Yourself in the Word of God

The Bible is the ultimate standard for truth and the plumb line against which all impressions must be tested. The more you know God's Word, the better equipped you are to identify anything that contradicts it.

- **Foundation of Truth:** Immerse yourself in Scripture daily. It sharpens your spiritual senses and provides the framework for sound judgment.

- **Transformative Meditation:** Don't just read; meditate on Scripture, allowing it to transform your mind (Romans 12:2). This builds a solid framework of truth against which all other information can be tested.

Fueling Your Spirit: Practice Consistent Prayer and Fasting These disciplines are powerful tools for spiritual sensitivity and authority.

- **Targeted Prayer:** Pray specifically for the gift of discernment (James 1:5). Ask God for clarity, wisdom, and revelation in specific situations.

- **Spiritual Sensitivity through Fasting:** Fasting sensitizes your spirit to the Holy Spirit's voice and breaks the power of the flesh, which can often cloud discernment. Jesus indicated that some "kind" only comes out by prayer and fasting (Mark 9:29).

Walking in Wisdom: Seek Wise Counsel and Accountability God designed us for community, and wisdom is often found in the multitude of counselors.

- **Mature Believers:** Surround yourself with mature, discerning believers who can offer biblical counsel and help you process impressions. "Where there is no counsel, the people fall; but in the multitude of counselors there is safety" (Proverbs 11:14).

- **Test Impressions:** Humbly share your discerned impressions with trusted spiritual leaders or mentors for confirmation or correction. Do not operate in isolation.

Growing Through Experience: Learn from Practice and Reflection Discernment grows with application and honest evaluation.

- **Post-Ministry Reflection:** After ministering, take time to reflect on what happened. What did you discern? Was it accurate? What could have been done differently?

- **Journaling Your Journey:** Keep a spiritual journal to record your discernments, their outcomes, and lessons learned. This helps you recognize patterns, track your growth, and build confidence in your spiritual senses.

Navigating the Minefield: Common Mistakes in Discernment

Even mature believers can fall into traps that hinder accurate discernment. Being aware of these pitfalls helps us walk in greater wisdom.

Over-Spiritualizing Every Problem: The "Demon Behind Every Bush" Trap

- **Mistake:** Attributing every negative event, struggle, or personality quirk solely to a demon. This can lead to misdirected efforts and neglect of natural or psychological issues.

- **Correction:** Remember the three sources of problems: the world, the flesh, and the devil. Not every illness is demonic; not every bad mood is a spirit of heaviness. Discern carefully, seeking the true root.

Fear-Based Discernment: When Fear Clouds Vision

- **Mistake:** Operating out of fear of demons, rather than out of faith in Christ's authority. Fear can distort perception, causing you to see demons where they are not, or to misinterpret genuine spiritual activity.

- **Correction:** "Perfect love casts out fear" (1 John 4:18). Approach deliverance from a place of God's love, power, and a sound mind (2 Timothy

1:7). Your authority is in Christ, not in your own strength.

Lacking Patience and Rushing: The Haste that Harms

- **Mistake:** Rushing into deliverance without taking sufficient time to discern the root cause, the specific "legal ground," or the Holy Spirit's precise leading.

- **Correction:** Discernment often requires patience and waiting on God's timing. Haste can lead to superficial or ineffective ministry, or even unintended consequences.

Operating Without Accountability: The Danger of Isolation

- **Mistake:** Attempting to discern and minister in isolation, without the input or covering of spiritual authority or a trusted team. This is a fertile ground for deception and pride.

- **Correction:** Humility dictates that we submit

our discernments to others for confirmation and wise counsel. This prevents pride, error, and burnout.

Relying Solely on Feelings: The Deception of Sensations

- **Mistake:** While the Holy Spirit may use feelings or physical sensations to communicate discernment, relying *solely* on them without biblical grounding or confirmation can lead to misinterpretation, as feelings can be deceptive.

- **Correction:** Always weigh impressions and sensations against Scripture. Seek confirmation through God's Word and the counsel of mature believers.

Discernment as a Lifestyle: Walking in Spiritual Clarity

Discernment is not just for "deliverance ministers"; it is a vital aspect of daily Christian living for every believer. It empowers you to navigate a spiritually charged world, identify the enemy's tactics, and walk in greater freedom and wisdom. By diligently cultivating this gift through intimacy with God, immersion in His Word, consistent prayer and fasting, and humble accountability, you will become a sharper instrument in the hands of the Deliverer, able to effectively discern and dismantle the works of darkness.

> "Solid food is for the mature, who by constant use have trained themselves to distinguish good from evil." —Hebrews 5:14

Next Chapter Preview: Physical Manifestations in Deliverance

Now that we've explored the crucial role of discernment, we'll turn our attention to a vital and often misunderstood area of deliverance ministry: physical manifestations. Understanding why demons manifest, how to respond with authority and compassion, and how to handle these moments with wisdom is key to safe and effective ministry.

Application Moment: Cultivate Spiritual Perception

1. **Reflect:**
   Are you discerning the spiritual source behind

situations, or reacting only to the natural?
Have you prayed for discernment or assumed your perspective was enough?

2. **Repent:**
"Holy Spirit, forgive me for leaning on human understanding. Sharpen my spiritual senses."

3. **Respond:**
Ask God daily for discernment. Begin to journal situations that feel "off" and invite the Spirit to reveal the root.
Declare:
"I will not be blind to spiritual realities. I receive God's discernment to walk wisely.

4. "

Chapter 14

THE ROLE OF PHYSICAL MANIFESTATIONS IN DELIVERANCE

In the ministry of deliverance, as vividly portrayed in Scripture and powerfully experienced today, the confrontation with evil spirits often leads to visible and audible manifestations as they are expelled. These reactions can range from subtle shifts in demeanor to dramatic physical expressions. Understanding the biblical precedent for such occurrences, why they happen, and how to respond appropriately is not just helpful—it is crucial for effective, sensitive, and safe deliverance ministry.

Step into the world of deliverance ministry, and you'll quickly realize this isn't just a matter of quiet prayers or gentle reassurances—sometimes, it's like witnessing a clash of kingdoms right in front of your eyes. When deliverance takes place, the evidence is often tangible, sometimes dramatic, unmistakably real. These moments are not just for the spiritually "elite"—they're meant to show every believer that the victory of Jesus over darkness is alive and active today.

You might see the slightest quiver in someone's expression, a sudden heaviness in the air, or even a change in their voice. Then there are the unmistakable moments—someone starts to shake, a sharp cry echoes through the room, or tears stream down a face as if a dam has burst. Some may cough, gag, or even physically tremble. While it may seem strange to those unfamiliar, these aren't simply emotional reactions— they're outward signs of an unseen conflict, a spiritual eviction in progress.

For anyone new to this, it's completely understandable to feel unsettled or even skeptical. But for those who've witnessed deliverance firsthand, these manifestations are powerful proof that freedom is happening in real time. They're not the focus, but they are the evidence— a sign that spiritual chains are being shattered and someone's life is being reclaimed from oppression.

Scripture is filled with these dramatic moments. Picture

men convulsing, voices crying out, people suddenly regaining speech or movement as Jesus commands freedom. These aren't dusty stories from ancient history—they're blueprints for what happens when faith collides with real-life need. They remind us that the power of Christ is not only relevant, but essential, for healing and wholeness today.

Being prepared for these moments matters. It's about having practical things on hand—a box of tissues, a trash can—but also about having a heart grounded in compassion and wisdom. The Holy Spirit's presence is your anchor, helping you navigate each situation with gentleness and authority (2 Timothy 1:7), never losing sight of the person at the center of it all.

At the end of the day, physical manifestations aren't about creating a spectacle—they're about declaring that light triumphs over darkness (John 1:5). When you witness a life set free, you're seeing God's heart for restoration in action. These moments, raw and unscripted as they may be, are a front-row invitation to see the impossible become possible, to witness hope breakthrough in places once ruled by despair.

One of the most eye-opening moments I encountered early in my journey with deliverance was during a church service. I remember walking into the sanctuary and noticing rolls of toilet paper placed along the front pews. At first, it seemed odd—unusual, even distracting. But what I witnessed next changed my understanding forever. People were being delivered before my eyes. It wasn't just emotional release—it was spiritual eviction. As prayer intensified, I saw individuals begin to gag, cough, and expel phlegm-like substances. The trash cans and tissues were not symbolic; they were tools of cleanup from a supernatural war being fought and won. I'll never forget the young woman who, in the midst of prayer, seemed calm and clear. Then suddenly, her face twisted, her body reacted violently, and she expelled a thick mass of phlegm. That moment marked her freedom. That moment revealed what it truly looks like when spiritual yokes break (Isaiah 10:27). These manifestations may appear strange or even disturbing to the untrained eye, but for those ministering in the authority of Jesus, they are critical indicators that real deliverance is taking place.

Echoes from Scripture: Biblical Precedents of Manifestations

The Gospels and the book of Acts provide numerous powerful accounts of physical manifestations occurring when Jesus and His disciples confronted evil spirits. These examples establish a clear, consistent biblical pattern, showing that such reactions are a natural part of demonic expulsion.

Jesus' encounters often involved dramatic physical reactions. We read of individuals experiencing convulsions and falling as demons were cast out. In Capernaum, a man with an unclean spirit cried out, and "when the demon had thrown him to the ground in front of everyone, it came out of him without doing him any harm" (Luke 4:35). Similarly, in Mark's account of the deaf and mute spirit, the demon, "shrieking and convulsing him violently, came out" (Mark 9:26).

Shrieking and crying out were common responses from demons, often acknowledging Jesus' identity and authority. "What do you want with us, Jesus of

Nazareth? Have you come to destroy us? I know who you are—the Holy One of God!" (Mark 1:24). These spirits frequently shrieked upon their departure, a sign of their forced eviction (Mark 9:26; Acts 8:7).

The afflicted often displayed disturbing physical signs. The boy with the deaf and mute spirit would frequently foam at the mouth and grind his teeth, becoming rigid (Mark 9:18). Sometimes, the very symptoms of demonic affliction would manifest dramatically upon the spirit's expulsion, such as loss of speech or hearing being immediately broken (Mark 9:25).

Demonic influence could also grant supernatural physical strength and violence. The Gerasene demoniac, for instance, exhibited immense strength, breaking chains and shackles, a stark example of demonic power manifesting physically (Mark 5:3-4). This spiritual torment could even manifest as hostility toward the presence of God, as seen in Mark 1:23-24, where a man possessed by an impure spirit interrupted Jesus in the synagogue with a cry of resistance. Self-harm and aggression could also be direct manifestations, as when Saul, afflicted by a distressing spirit, attempted to murder David with a spear (1 Samuel 18:10–11).

Beyond these, chronic disease could be tied to a spirit. Luke 13:11 records a woman who had "a spirit of infirmity for eighteen years" and was physically bent over. Jesus identified her prolonged condition as demonic in nature, and her healing came through deliverance. While not explicitly detailed in every account, the overall impression is often one of distress, contortion, or an unnatural voice as the spirit resists. These biblical accounts demonstrate that manifestations are a natural, though not always present, part of demonic expulsion. They serve as a clear sign that a spiritual entity is being confronted and forced to leave.

Why the Unseen Becomes Visible: Understanding Manifestations Today

When a demonic spirit is confronted with the authority of Jesus Christ (Luke 10:19), it is forced to react. Manifestations are often a sign of the spirit's desperate resistance, its attempt to intimidate, or its unavoidable forced departure.

- **Resistance and Intimidation:** Demons do not want to leave their "habitation" (Matthew 12:43). Manifestations can be a last-ditch effort to resist the command, distract the ministers, or instill fear in the person being ministered to or those witnessing the deliverance. It's a spiritual tantrum designed to maintain control.

- **Forced Departure:** As the spirit is compelled to leave, it may cause physical reactions in the host body as it exits. This is akin to a parasite being forcibly removed from a body, causing a physical reaction in the host.

- **Revealing Identity:** Sometimes, a manifestation (e.g., a specific voice, a violent reaction, or a particular physical contortion) can reveal the nature or even the name of the spirit, aiding the deliverance team in its expulsion (Mark 5:9).

- **Physical Symptoms of Affliction:** If the demon was causing a physical symptom (e.g., muteness, pain, or a specific illness), the body may react as that spiritual influence is broken, often with a final convulsion or expulsion of some kind.

- **Varying Degrees:** It's important to remember that manifestations can vary greatly in intensity. They might be as subtle as yawning, coughing, burping, or a slight twitch. More intense expressions can include shaking, screaming, vomiting, or convulsions. Some report a purging of mucus or phlegm—common in expelling spirits rooted in defilement or infirmity. These expulsions are not merely symbolic; they often indicate a physical release tied to a spiritual break. Not everyone being delivered will manifest overtly, but the absence of a visible manifestation does not mean deliverance hasn't occurred.

The Enemy's Disguises: Categories of Manifestations

Demonic spirits can manifest through various channels, impacting the physical, mental, emotional, and even moral aspects of a person's life. Recognizing these categories helps in discerning and addressing the specific influence.

Physical Manifestations: The Body's Reaction Demons often manifest through involuntary physical reactions in a person's body. These can include:

- Convulsions or shaking (Mark 9:20)
- Involuntary vomiting, coughing, gagging, spitting, or expulsion of phlegm-like substances
- Eyes rolling back, unnatural facial contortions, or foaming at the mouth
- Sudden, inexplicable surges of strength or violence. This was dramatically seen when a single demon-possessed man overpowered seven sons of Sceva, revealing supernatural strength beyond human capability (Acts 19:13-16).
- Temporary paralysis or muteness (Mark 9:25)
- Unusual body odors or sensations (e.g., cold spots, tingling).

Mental and Emotional Manifestations: The Battle for the Mind Demonic spirits frequently attack the mind and emotions, producing profound distress:

- Severe depression, chronic anxiety, and persistent suicidal thoughts (e.g., Psalm 42:11)
- Irrational fears, phobias, and panic attacks (e.g., 2 Timothy 1:7)
- Compulsive behaviors, obsessions, and uncontrollable urges
- Hearing voices (auditory hallucinations) or experiencing schizophrenia-like symptoms that defy natural explanation
- Periods of insanity, confusion, or double-mindedness (James 1:8).

Moral and Behavioral Manifestations: Corrupting Conduct Demonic spirits can manifest through consistent patterns of ungodly behavior that seem beyond a person's natural control:

- Addictions (alcohol, drugs, pornography, food, gambling) (e.g., Romans 6:16)
- Uncontrollable lust or perversion (e.g., 1 Corinthians 6:18)
- Chronic anger, rage, and violence (e.g., Ephesians 4:26-27)

- Persistent lying or deceitful behavior (e.g., John 8:44)
- Deep-seated rebellion or antisocial conduct (e.g., 1 Samuel 15:23).

Religious Manifestations: Counterfeit Spirituality
Some demons manifest in false spiritual expressions or reactions to genuine spiritual activity:

- False tongues or counterfeit spiritual manifestations that do not align with the Holy Spirit (e.g., 1 Corinthians 14:33).
- Disruptive behavior during worship, preaching, or prayer meetings.
- Mocking or blasphemous speech directed at God or sacred things (e.g., Mark 3:29).
- An inability to say the name of Jesus or quote Scripture.
- Displaying supernatural knowledge or counterfeit prophecy that is not from God (e.g., Acts 16:16-18).

Occult and Supernatural Manifestations: When Forbidden Doors Open These manifestations occur when a person has engaged with occult practices (as discussed in Chapter 8), creating direct access for spirits:

- Unexplained psychic abilities or clairvoyance
- Experiences of astral projection or seeing spirits
- Involuntary trances or blackouts
- Poltergeist-like activity (objects moving or voices heard without physical cause)
- Strong aversion or violent reaction to sacred items (e.g., crosses, Bibles, anointing oil).

Ministering Through the Storm: Practical and Sensitive Guidance

Handling manifestations requires a delicate but firm balance of spiritual authority, profound compassion, practical wisdom, and an unwavering commitment to safety. The ultimate goal is always the person's freedom and holistic wholeness, not sensationalism or drama.

Maintaining Authority and Calm:

- **Stay in Charge:** The minister, operating in Christ's authority (Luke 10:19), must remain calm, confident, and firmly in control of the situation. Do not be intimidated, distracted, or drawn into conversation by the manifestations.

- **Speak to the Spirit, Not the Person:** Address the demon directly, commanding it in Jesus' name (Mark 16:17), rather than engaging in conversation with the manifesting person. Remember, the person is not the demon.

- **Avoid Sensationalism:** Never encourage, prolong, or provoke manifestations for dramatic effect. The focus is solely on the spirit's departure and the person's liberation, not its display.

Ensuring Safety and Dignity:

- **Physical Safety:** If the person is thrashing, convulsing, or attempting self-harm, ensure they do not injure themselves or others. Have trusted team members gently hold them or guide them to a safe position (e.g., lying down on the floor). Remove any sharp objects or obstacles from the vicinity.

- **Confidentiality and Privacy:** Conduct deliverance in a private, confidential setting, especially if dramatic manifestations are anticipated (Proverbs 11:13).
- **Dignity and Respect:** Always treat the person with profound respect and compassion (Colossians 3:12), even when a demon is manifesting through them. Cover them with a blanket if clothing becomes disheveled. Speak kindly and reassuringly to the person, reminding them of God's love.

Specific Responses to Common Manifestations:

- **Coughing/Gagging/Vomiting/Spitting/ Phlegm Expulsion:** These are common ways spirits exit. Have a bucket, tissues, or towels readily available. Do not be alarmed; these are often clear signs of release and a spiritual purge.
- **Shrieking or Screaming:** Command the spirit to be silent in Jesus' name, just as Jesus often did (Mark 1:25).
- **Convulsing or Thrashing:** Gently but firmly stabilize the person to prevent injury, while

continuing to command the spirit to leave with authority.

- **Mocking or Laughing:** Do not engage in dialogue with the spirit. Simply rebuke it and continue with authoritative commands for it to leave.
- **Physical Pain or Pressure:** Command the spirit causing the pain to leave. The pain often subsides immediately as the spirit departs.

The Importance of Trauma-Informed Approaches:

- **Interplay with Trauma:** It's vital to recognize that physical manifestations can sometimes trigger or be deeply intertwined with past physical, emotional, or sexual trauma. The body may react in ways that mirror past abuse or fear, even if the primary issue is demonic.
- **Sensitivity and Care:** Ministers must be highly sensitive and compassionate (Ephesians 4:32). If a person has a history of trauma, manifestations might be particularly distressing for them.

- **Creating a Safe Space:** Ensure the person feels safe, heard, and respected throughout the process. Prioritize their emotional and physical well-being above all else.

- **Pacing the Process:** Sometimes, it's necessary to slow down the deliverance process, allow the person to process emotions, or even pause deliverance to address trauma through inner healing (as discussed in Chapter 9B) before proceeding with further spiritual confrontation.

After the Battle: Post-Manifestation Care and Follow-Up

Once a spirit has departed and manifestations cease, the person may feel exhausted, disoriented, or emotionally raw. This immediate aftercare is crucial for sealing the breakthrough and preventing re-entry.

Comfort and Reassurance: Offer immediate comfort, reassurance, and a sense of peace (2 Corinthians 1:3-4). Remind them of their identity and victory in Christ (Romans 8:37). Affirm their freedom (John 8:36). **The Infilling of the Spirit:** Immediately encourage the person to invite the Holy Spirit to fill any void left by the departing spirit (Ephesians 5:18). Lead them in prayer to receive more of God's presence, peace, joy, and love. This is vital to prevent the "empty house" scenario (Matthew 12:43-45). **Addressing Practical Needs:** Offer water, a blanket, or a quiet space to rest if needed. Provide tissues or a bucket for any lingering physical expulsions. **Sustaining Freedom:** Emphasize the importance of the principles outlined in Chapter 10 ("Be Intentional – Getting and Maintaining Your Deliverance"). Schedule follow-up conversations to ensure they are integrating their freedom, building new habits, and staying connected to a supportive community (Hebrews 10:25).

Authority with Compassion

Physical manifestations in deliverance are not to be sought for their own sake, nor are they to be feared. They are simply a reality of confronting unseen evil and a powerful sign of God's triumph over it (1 John 3:8). By understanding their biblical basis, recognizing their purpose, and approaching them with a blend of unwavering spiritual authority (Mark 16:17) and profound compassion (Colossians 3:12), ministers can effectively facilitate freedom while honoring the dignity and well-being of the individual. The ultimate focus remains on the person's complete liberation and their journey into holistic wholeness in Christ.

Sustaining Your Freedom: What Comes Next?

Now that we've addressed the practicalities of manifestations, we will broaden our scope to consider deliverance in various specific contexts. In the next chapter, we will explore unique considerations when ministering to children, addressing family strongholds, establishing church-based ministries, and working alongside mental health professionals.

Application Moment: Focus on the Fruit, Not the Flash

1. **Reflect:**
   Have you misunderstood or feared physical manifestations during deliverance—such as shaking, weeping, or speaking out?
   Do you recognize that true deliverance is marked by lasting fruit, not just emotional moments?

2. **Repent:**
   "Lord, forgive me for focusing on the dramatic

*rather than the redemptive. Teach me to trust
Your Spirit, not spectacle."*

3. **Respond:**
   Write down what fruit you want to see in your
   life (peace, joy, clarity).
   Declare:
   *"I receive lasting freedom, not just outward
   signs. My deliverance will bear the fruit of the
   Spirit."*

Chapter 15

A COMPASSIONATE APPROACH

DELIVERANCE FOR EVERY HEART AND HOME

The journey to freedom in Christ, while deeply personal, rarely happens in isolation. Our lives are woven into families, communities, and broader societal contexts, each with its own unique dynamics and vulnerabilities. While the core principles of deliverance remain steadfast, the art of applying them effectively demands wisdom, discernment, and a profound compassion tailored to the individual's specific situation. This chapter explores how the liberating power of Christ can be brought to bear in diverse settings, from the tender hearts of children to the complex landscape of mental health, and within the very fabric of our churches and families.

Whispers of Freedom for Little Ones: Ministering to Children

Imagine a child, perhaps restless at night, plagued by nightmares, or displaying sudden, inexplicable behavioral shifts that defy typical explanations. While a parent's first thought might be a phase or a medical issue, the spiritual realm can sometimes play a role, especially given that many "demonic issues start as early as the womb – 5 years old," when children are most impressionable and vulnerable. Their developing understanding, heightened sensitivity, and limited ability to articulate deep spiritual distress make them unique recipients of deliverance.

Understanding Their Tender Vulnerabilities
Children are like open sponges, absorbing everything around them (Proverbs 22:6). This includes the echoes of family trauma, inherited generational patterns (Exodus 20:5), or even subtle exposures to ungodly themes in media, games, or play. Their innocence, though beautiful, can also mean they lack the developed discernment and spiritual defenses of an adult, making them particularly susceptible to spiritual influence.

They often express spiritual distress through physical symptoms, behavioral issues, or vivid nightmares, as their young minds may not yet grasp complex spiritual concepts.

A Gentle Hand and a Loving Heart When ministering to a child, the approach must be steeped in immense sensitivity and protection. Always, *always* secure explicit consent from parents or legal guardians, and ideally, have them present, as their authority is vital (Ephesians 6:4). Speak simply, focusing on Jesus' boundless love, His power to make them happy and free from anything "bad," and His role as their protector (Psalm 91:4). Avoid any language or actions that could frighten or traumatize the child. Use analogies they can understand, like "Jesus wants to help you get rid of the yucky feeling inside" or "Jesus is stronger than any scary thing." Creating a calm, reassuring atmosphere is paramount.

Speaking Truth into Their World Help the child (or the parents on their behalf) confess any known "bad choices," renounce ungodly influences (such as exposure to occultic cartoons or games), and choose to forgive anyone who has hurt them (Matthew 18:21-22). Immediately after, lead them into inviting the Holy Spirit to fill them with peace and joy, reinforcing that Jesus is now their protector and friend. Ongoing discipleship, consistent prayer, and a godly home environment are their best safeguards for sustained freedom, building a strong spiritual foundation (Proverbs 22:6).

Unraveling the Threads of the Past: Deliverance for Families

Have you ever noticed patterns repeating in your family—a cycle of divorce, chronic illness, financial struggle, or a particular sin that seems to cling to every generation? These aren't always coincidences; they can be the tell-tale signs of family strongholds, invisible chains that bind entire households (Lamentations 5:7). The enemy thrives on these inherited "legal grounds," perpetuating dysfunction across the family tree.

Identifying the Echoes: Discerning Family Patterns
The first step is to discern these recurring patterns. Is

there a history of addiction, anger, or broken relationships that transcends individual personalities? Are there ungodly soul ties—unhealthy emotional or sexual bonds—that drain life from family members? Are there ancestral sins or curses (as discussed in Chapter 15) that have never been broken, continuing to impact the present generation (Exodus 20:5)? This requires careful, prayerful observation and sometimes, a review of family history.

A Collective Journey to Freedom: Breaking Generational Bonds Family deliverance is a powerful act of collective repentance and breaking. It involves:

- **Corporate Confession:** Family members coming together to confess ancestral sins and ungodly patterns that have afflicted their lineage (Leviticus 26:40). This shared act of humility and repentance is deeply liberating.

- **Breaking Curses:** Utilizing the principles of Chapter 15 (Breaking Curses and Releasing Blessings) to specifically dismantle generational curses that have held the family captive

(Galatians 3:13). This is done through the authority of Christ's finished work on the cross.

- **Renouncing Legacies:** Verbally renouncing any ungodly beliefs, practices, or inheritances of darkness passed down through the family line, declaring allegiance solely to Christ (Acts 19:18-19).

- **Radical Forgiveness:** Facilitating forgiveness among family members for past hurts, opening the door for healing and reconciliation within the household (Ephesians 4:32). This breaks the legal right of tormenting spirits.

- **Rededicating the Home:** A corporate act of dedicating their home and family to Jesus Christ, inviting His Lordship and protection to fill every room and establish a new spiritual atmosphere of peace and holiness (Joshua 24:15).

- **Building New Foundations:** Committing to establishing new, godly habits of communication, prayer, and mutual support, intentionally replacing the old, destructive patterns with Christ-centered ones (Ephesians

4:22-24). This ensures the "house" remains filled and guarded.

A Safe Harbor for Healing: Deliverance in the Church Setting

For the ministry of deliverance to truly flourish and be sustained, it must find its home within the local church. The church, as the body of Christ, is designed to be a safe harbor where individuals can find not only salvation but also complete liberation (Ephesians 4:11-13). This requires intentional leadership, thorough training, and clear, compassionate protocols.

The Shepherd's Heart: Leadership and Vision

Deliverance ministry must be embraced and championed by the senior pastoral leadership (Hebrews 13:17). It's not a fringe activity but a core expression of the Gospel—Jesus came to "set at liberty those who are oppressed" (Luke 4:18). A clear vision, rooted in sound biblical theology, must be communicated to the entire congregation, dispelling fear and fostering faith in God's power to deliver. Pastors are called to equip the saints for the work of ministry (Ephesians 4:12), and this includes spiritual warfare.

Equipping the Saints: Training and Preparation
Building an effective deliverance ministry means carefully selecting and comprehensively training a team of mature, discerning, and compassionate believers (2 Timothy 2:2). Their training should cover:

- Biblical understanding of spiritual warfare and demonology (Ephesians 6:12).

- Sharpening discernment (as discussed in Chapter 11), to accurately identify spiritual roots.

- Practical steps for ministry, including handling manifestations safely and discreetly (as discussed in Chapter 12).

- Inner healing techniques (from Chapter 9), recognizing the interconnectedness of soul wounds and spiritual bondage.

- Crucially, robust post-deliverance care and discipleship, to ensure sustained freedom (Matthew 12:43-45).

- Emphasis on strict confidentiality and healthy boundaries, protecting both the recipient and the ministers (Proverbs 11:13).

Order and Integrity: Establishing Protocols Clear protocols are vital for the integrity and effectiveness of the ministry. This includes a confidential intake process to understand the individual's history and specific needs, always ministering in teams (Ecclesiastes 4:9-12; preferably same-gender for the recipient), and ensuring a strong follow-up system to integrate individuals into the church community. Deliverance should never stand alone but be woven into the broader fabric of pastoral care, counseling, and small group discipleship, fostering a culture of holistic healing and freedom.

Walking the Fine Line: Deliverance and Mental Health Challenges

One of the most sensitive and crucial areas of ministry lies at the intersection of spiritual deliverance and mental health. It is an absolute imperative to understand that **deliverance ministry does not replace professional mental health care.** Instead, it can work powerfully *in conjunction* with it, offering a holistic path to healing.

Discerning the Roots: Spiritual vs. Medical Not every mental health struggle is demonic. Many conditions like clinical depression, anxiety disorders, or bipolar disorder have biological, psychological, and environmental components. It is irresponsible and harmful to attribute all mental illness solely to demons. However, demonic spirits are opportunistic; they can exploit existing mental vulnerabilities, exacerbate symptoms, or even mimic mental illness. Discernment (Chapter 11) is paramount here. When in doubt, always, *always* err on the side of caution and recommend a medical or psychological evaluation. Ministers should humbly acknowledge their limitations and seek multidisciplinary approaches (Proverbs 11:14).

The Power of Collaboration: Working Together for Wholeness The most effective approach often involves collaboration between spiritual and medical professionals. Deliverance ministers should be prepared to refer individuals to qualified Christian counselors, therapists, or psychiatrists when mental health issues are suspected or diagnosed. Ideally, a person receiving spiritual deliverance for oppression might also be simultaneously engaged in professional therapy for trauma, anxiety, or depression. Ministers must respect professional boundaries, focusing on the spiritual aspects without attempting to diagnose or treat medical conditions. The goal is the person's complete well-being, utilizing all available resources.

Compassion Over Condemnation: A Heart of Understanding Above all, minister to those with mental health challenges with profound patience, understanding, and compassion (Colossians 3:12). Never condemn or shame someone, implying their struggle is due to a lack of faith or unconfessed sin. The goal is holistic wholeness—spiritual, emotional, and physical—and sometimes, that requires a multi-faceted approach involving both spiritual and medical professionals. The church should be a place of refuge and support, not judgment, for those battling mental health issues (Galatians 6:2).

Tailoring Ministry for Greater Impact

The liberating power of Jesus Christ is for everyone, in every circumstance. By understanding the unique dynamics and vulnerabilities within different contexts—whether ministering to a child, addressing a family stronghold, establishing a church-wide ministry, or collaborating wisely with mental health professionals—ministers can apply biblical principles with greater precision, sensitivity, and ultimately, greater impact. This tailored, compassionate approach ensures that freedom is not only gained but also sustained, leading to deeper and more lasting transformation in individual hearts and across entire homes.

Sustaining Your Freedom: What Comes Next?

Having explored how deliverance applies in specific personal and relational contexts, we will now broaden our understanding of spiritual warfare beyond individual liberation. In the next chapter, we will delve into engaging in corporate spiritual warfare, understanding territorial spirits, breaking strongholds over communities, and the profound power of intercessory deliverance for others.

Application Moment: Love as the Foundation

1. **Reflect:**
   Do you view others with compassion when they struggle—or with criticism and pride?
   Have you been wounded by unkind deliverance practices?

2. **Repent:**
   "Jesus, forgive me for lacking compassion toward others—or for not receiving grace myself."

3. **Respond:**
   Commit to show compassion in how you speak, minister, and pray.
   Declare:
   "I will be an agent of freedom rooted in love, not pride or fear."

Chapter 16

DELIVERANCE FOR CHILDREN AND TEENS SAFEGUARDING THE NEXT GENERATION

> "From infancy you have known the Holy Scriptures, which are able to make you wise for salvation through faith in Christ Jesus." —2 Timothy 3:15

The Battle Begins Early and Touches Every Home

Parents often grapple with concerning and frightening behaviors in their children, wondering about the root cause. Could it be a phase, a psychological issue, or something more? Children and teenagers are not exempt from spiritual warfare. In fact, the enemy often targets the young because of their vulnerability, impressionability, and profound prophetic potential. Throughout Scripture, God calls and uses youth—

Samuel serving in the temple from a tender age (1 Samuel 2:18), David as a shepherd boy chosen to be king (1 Samuel 16:11-13), Jeremiah called as a prophet from his mother's womb (Jeremiah 1:5), and even John the Baptist leaping in Elizabeth's womb, filled with the Holy Spirit (Luke 1:41). Yet, just as God seeks to mark children for His divine purposes, the enemy relentlessly seeks to mark them for destruction. Deliverance ministry must therefore include acute awareness, sharp discernment, and compassionate intervention for young people, ensuring they walk in the full freedom Christ intended.

When Darkness Touches Innocence: Biblical Foundations for Deliverance in Children

Scripture does not shy away from showing children under demonic influence, providing clear precedents for their need for deliverance and Jesus' authority to set them free. These accounts remind us that age is no barrier to spiritual affliction, nor to divine liberation.

One poignant example is found in **Mark 9:17–27** (also Luke 9:37-42), where a desperate father brings his son to Jesus. This boy was tormented by a mute and convulsing spirit, often thrown into fire and water, suffering greatly from childhood. The disciples had failed to deliver him, highlighting the need for true authority and faith (Mark 9:18-19). Jesus, with a powerful word, cast out the demon, and the boy was instantly restored. This narrative underscores that children *can* indeed be demonized, and that Jesus *has authority* to deliver them—an authority He delegates to His followers.

Similarly, in **Matthew 15:21–28**, a Canaanite woman, a Gentile, pleads with Jesus for her daughter, who is described as "severely demon-possessed." Despite initial testing of her faith, Jesus responds to her persistence, and the daughter is delivered remotely, simply by Jesus' word spoken from a distance. This again affirms that children are targets of demonic activity and that Jesus' power transcends physical proximity.

Even anointed individuals can suffer under oppression, as seen with young King Saul in **1 Samuel 16:14**. Though not a child, Saul was afflicted by a distressing spirit from the Lord, demonstrating how spiritual torment can manifest even in leaders. This serves as a broader biblical principle that spiritual affliction can touch anyone, regardless of age or position, if doors are opened.

These passages highlight two crucial truths for our understanding today:

- Children, from infancy through their teenage years, *can* be demonized or afflicted by evil spirits.
- Jesus *has absolute authority* to deliver them— and He has commissioned and empowered His followers to carry on this ministry (Mark 16:17).

Vulnerable Hearts, Open Doors: Common Gateways to Demonic Influence in Youth

Children and teenagers, due to their developing minds, emotional sensitivities, and exposure to various influences, can become demonically influenced through several common gateways. Understanding these entry points is vital for identifying and closing them, protecting the next generation from the enemy's schemes.

Generational Echoes: Curses and Family Sin

Children are deeply connected to their family lineage. Unrepented sin, spiritual rebellion, or occult involvement in a household can pass down familiar spirits or predispositions to certain strongholds (Exodus 20:5). Children born into families steeped in occult practices, addiction, perversion, or chronic dysfunction often carry spiritual residue or vulnerabilities that make them susceptible to similar patterns. They may inherit a "legal ground" for demonic influence without any active participation on their part (Lamentations 5:7). This highlights the importance of family deliverance (as discussed in Chapter 13).

Wounds of the Past: Early Exposure to Trauma

Trauma creates deep wounds in the soul, which can serve as significant entry points for demonic oppression (Psalm 147:3). Children and teens are particularly vulnerable to:

- **Abuse:** Sexual, verbal, emotional, or physical abuse can leave lasting scars that spirits of shame, fear, rejection, or defilement exploit. The emotional pain can become a "foothold" (Ephesians 4:27) for tormenting spirits.

- **Abandonment or Adoption Trauma:** The deep wound of feeling unwanted or disconnected can open doors to spirits of abandonment and insecurity, leading to lifelong struggles with identity and belonging.

- **Exposure to Violence or Instability:** Witnessing domestic violence, living in chaotic environments, or experiencing profound instability can create fear-based strongholds and a constant sense of dread (2 Timothy 1:7).

- **Direct Exposure to Witchcraft:** Children raised in homes where witchcraft or occult practices are present are often directly exposed to demonic influence, inheriting spiritual ties and open doors.

The Digital Gates: Media and Technology

In today's digital age, media and technology have become pervasive gateways, often without parents realizing the spiritual implications. Children and teens may unintentionally open doors through content that glorifies darkness:

- **Dark Games and Horror Films:** Video games with occult themes, horror films, anime with spiritualistic elements, or virtual spaces with avatars, portals, or summoning rituals can introduce unclean spirits into their lives (Deuteronomy 18:10-12). These can normalize or even invite demonic interaction.

- **Social Media Trends:** Popular social media trends or challenges (e.g., playing with Ouija boards, "light as a feather, stiff as a board," "Bloody Mary" rituals) can be direct invitations for demonic activity, often undertaken out of curiosity or peer pressure, but with very real spiritual consequences.

Entangled Souls: Ungodly Ties and Peer Influence

As young people navigate friendships and relationships, they form deep emotional and spiritual connections.

- **Unholy Soul Ties:** Children and teens can form ungodly soul ties through unhealthy friendships, manipulative relationships, or premature sexual experiences, including sexting or exposure to pornography. These ties act as conduits for shared demonic oppression, transferring spiritual burdens or influences (1 Corinthians 6:16-17).
- **Peer Pressure:** The intense desire for acceptance and belonging can lead young people into activities that open spiritual doors, even if they intuitively feel something is wrong (Proverbs 1:10-16).

Recognizing the Shadows: Signs of Demonic Oppression in Young Lives

Identifying demonic oppression in children and teens requires careful discernment, as some behaviors can mimic normal developmental stages or psychological issues. However, certain persistent or extreme behaviors, especially when combined with other indicators, may point to deeper spiritual issues at play. This is where wise parents and ministers must seek the Holy Spirit's guidance.

Look for patterns such as:

- **Sudden, Drastic Personality Changes:** Uncharacteristic rage, violence, extreme defiance, or withdrawal that is unexplainable by natural means.
- **Suicidal Ideation or Self-Harm:** Persistent thoughts of suicide, or engaging in self-harming behaviors like cutting or burning, often accompanied by isolation and despair (Psalm 34:18).
- **Unexplained Aversion to Spiritual Things:** An unusual or intense fear of Scripture, worship music, prayer, church, or even mentioning the name of Jesus (John 1:5).
- **Persistent Night Terrors or Recurring Nightmares:** Especially those involving dark

figures, monsters, or a sense of being tormented, leading to chronic sleep disturbance.

- **Drawing Dark or Demonic Figures:** A preoccupation with, or unexplained compulsion to draw, disturbing or occultic imagery.

- **Involvement in Occult Paraphernalia:** A sudden, uncharacteristic interest in crystals, tarot cards, Ouija boards, or other spiritual paraphernalia.

- **Unexplained Physical Ailments:** Chronic health issues that defy medical diagnosis or treatment, sometimes linked to a spirit of infirmity (Luke 13:11).

- **Specific Oppressive Behaviors:** Manifestations of spirits of murder, violence, hiding, fear of death, rebellion, anger, or deep-seated abandonment and rejection that seem beyond a child's natural temperament.

It's profoundly important to distinguish between natural emotional development (e.g., mood swings in puberty), genuine psychological issues (e.g., clinical depression, anxiety disorders), and genuine spiritual bondage.

These are not mutually exclusive—and often coexist. Discernment (Chapter 11) is paramount, and collaboration with mental health professionals (Chapter 13) is often wise, ensuring a holistic approach to the child's well-being.

A Gentle Hand, A Powerful Spirit: Ministering Deliverance to Young People

Delivering children and teens requires immense discernment, profound compassion, and great care. The approach must be tailored to their age and understanding, always prioritizing their safety and long-term wholeness.

Covering the Home: The Spiritual Foundation

Deliverance for a child often begins with **deliverance for the parent or guardian**. Spiritual headship matters (Ephesians 6:4). When the home environment is spiritually unclean, divided by strife, or marked by unconfessed sin, the child remains vulnerable.

- **Proverbs 3:33** states, "The curse of the Lord is on the house of the wicked, but He blesses the home of the just." A clean and consecrated home creates a protective spiritual atmosphere, a sanctuary for the child.

- Parents must be willing to repent for their own sins, renounce ungodly patterns, and dedicate their household to Christ (Joshua 24:15). This act of spiritual leadership provides a powerful covering for their children.

Age-Appropriate Ministry: Tailoring the Approach
The way you minister must align with the child's developmental stage, ensuring understanding and minimizing fear:

- **Children Under 7:** Keep language simple and direct. Focus on Jesus' boundless love and power. Pray over them, gently lay hands on them, and speak Scripture aloud (Mark 10:16). Avoid detailed explanations of demons that might frighten them. They primarily need the spiritual authority of adults to intercede on their behalf.
- **Ages 8–12:** Begin to involve them more directly. Allow them to express feelings and ask gentle questions about anything scary or wrong that has

happened. Explain deliverance in simple terms (e.g., "Jesus wants to help you get rid of the yucky feeling that is bothering you"). Lead them in simple prayers of confession and renunciation (Romans 10:10).

- **Teens (13+):** Engage them more fully in the process. Explain deliverance clearly, ensuring they understand what is happening. Ask for their explicit agreement and willingness to participate (Joshua 24:15). Confession and renunciation of their own sins and past involvements become increasingly important, as does their commitment to post-deliverance disciplines.

Teaching Identity and Authority: Equipping for Life

Young people must know they are not defined by trauma or torment, but by their identity in Christ. This foundational truth empowers them to walk in lasting freedom. Equip them to:

- **Know the Truth of God's Word:** Teach them who they are in Christ (2 Corinthians 5:17) and about God's unconditional love for them

(Jeremiah 31:3). This truth sets them free (John 8:32).

- **Renounce Fear, Shame, and Guilt:** Guide them to verbally reject the lies of the enemy and embrace God's truth about their forgiveness and acceptance (Romans 8:1).

- **Declare Freedom through Christ:** Teach them to use their own voice to declare their freedom and authority in Jesus' name (Luke 10:19), actively resisting the enemy (James 4:7).

D. Post-Deliverance Discipleship: Sustaining the Breakthrough Freedom, once gained, must be followed by intentional discipleship and a commitment to new habits (Matthew 12:43-45). This is crucial for sustained liberty.

- **New Spiritual Habits:** Encourage consistent prayer, worship, and Bible reading (Chapter 10). These disciplines fill the "empty house" with God's presence.

- **Parental Reinforcement:** Parents play a crucial role in reinforcing the child's freedom, speaking life over them, and maintaining a godly home environment (Proverbs 22:6).

- **Church Community Support:** Ensure the young person is connected to a supportive, Bible-believing youth group or church community (Hebrews 10:25). This provides a network of encouragement, accountability, and continued spiritual growth.

A Story of Breakthrough: Hope for the Tormented

I remember a 13-year-old girl who suffered nightly terror. Her mother brought her to our church, convinced it was just a phase of adolescence. During prayer, however, it became clear she was tormented by something unseen, manifesting as extreme fear and nightmares. We later learned she had been watching spiritual summoning videos on YouTube and had begun drawing pentagrams and dark figures out of curiosity. Over several weeks, we prayed with her, led her in renouncing those ungodly agreements, and immersed her in worship and the Word of God. Her peace returned. Today, she testifies of God's power, sings in worship, and mentors younger girls, a living testament to Christ's delivering power.

Raising a Shield: Proactive Safeguarding in the Church

The Church has a vital role in protecting and preparing the next generation for spiritual warfare. This involves proactive measures and intentional ministry, creating a safe and empowering environment.

- **Train Children's and Youth Workers:** Equip those who minister to young people with foundational understanding of spiritual warfare, discernment, and basic deliverance principles. This ensures they can recognize and respond appropriately to spiritual issues.
- **Maintain Spiritually Clean Environments:** Regularly consecrate and cleanse children's and youth ministry spaces to God, ensuring they are free from any defiled objects or ungodly influences (Acts 19:19).
- **Listen to Children's Cries:** Don't dismiss children's fears, confusion, or unusual

behaviors. Listen with a discerning ear, taking their spiritual experiences seriously and responding with prayer and wisdom (James 1:5).

- **Encourage Spiritual Disciplines:** Foster a culture that encourages fasting, prayer, and intentional intercession for students, equipping them with spiritual weapons from a young age (Ephesians 6:10-18).

Freedom for the Little Ones

> **"Let the little children come to Me, and do not forbid them; for of such is the kingdom of heaven." —Matthew 19:14**

Jesus' invitation to children underscores their profound value in God's Kingdom. Deliverance is not just for adults burdened with years of sin—it's also for the young, whom Jesus treasures deeply. By removing the footholds of darkness early, we empower a generation to rise in light, strength, and wholeness. When children are delivered, homes are healed, destinies are restored, and future cycles of bondage are broken, impacting generations for Christ.

Looking Ahead Having explored how deliverance applies to children and teens, we will now broaden our understanding to the full scope of spiritual warfare. In Chapter 17: Kingdom Advance: Warfare for Territories and Peoples, we will delve into engaging in corporate spiritual warfare, understanding territorial spirits, breaking strongholds over communities, and the profound power of intercessory deliverance for others.

Application Moment: A Heart Check for Ministry

As you prepare to minister to the next generation—or reflect on your own experiences—pause and allow the Holy Spirit to examine your heart.

1. **Reflect**
   Do you view others with compassion when they struggle—or with criticism and pride?
   Have you been wounded by unkind deliverance practices?

2. **Repent**

"Jesus, forgive me for lacking compassion toward others—or for not receiving grace myself."

3. **3. Respond**

Commit to show compassion in how you speak, minister, and pray.
Declare: "I will be an agent of freedom rooted in love, not pride or fear."

Chapter 17

KINGDOM ADVANCE: WARFARE FOR TERRITORIES AND PEOPLES

Our journey through deliverance has primarily focused on personal freedom and the liberation of individuals and their immediate families. However, the scope of spiritual warfare extends far beyond the individual. The Bible reveals a vast, unseen conflict impacting communities, regions, and even nations. Just as Jesus commissioned His disciples to cast out demons from individuals, He also called them to advance His Kingdom, which inherently involves confronting and dismantling corporate strongholds of darkness. This chapter will explore how believers can engage in spiritual warfare on a broader scale, understanding territorial spirits, breaking corporate strongholds, and practicing intercessory deliverance for others.

The Unseen Battlegrounds: Understanding Territorial Spirits

Imagine an unseen battlefront, where spiritual forces vie for influence over specific geographical areas, shaping the very atmosphere, cultures, and even political landscapes of those regions. This is the profound concept of "territorial spirits," deeply rooted in the biblical narrative, revealing that spiritual battles are often fought over specific domains.

One of the clearest biblical glimpses into this reality is found in the book of Daniel. The prophet Daniel was engaged in fervent prayer and fasting, seeking understanding, when the angel Gabriel appeared to him. Gabriel revealed that he had been delayed for 21 days by the **"prince of the kingdom of Persia"** (Daniel 10:13, 20). This wasn't a human king, but a high-ranking demonic entity resisting God's messenger and hindering the spiritual breakthrough Daniel was praying for. This powerful encounter reveals a spiritual hierarchy, suggesting that specific demonic powers are assigned to nations or regions, influencing their spiritual climate and resisting divine intervention. Daniel also mentions the "prince of Greece," further solidifying this understanding that nations have spiritual adversaries.

The Apostle Paul further illuminates this reality, declaring that our struggle is not against "flesh and blood, but against **principalities, against powers, against the rulers of the darkness of this age, against spiritual hosts of wickedness in the heavenly places**" (Ephesians 6:12). These terms paint a vivid picture of an organized, hierarchical demonic structure, with varying ranks of authority. These forces exert influence over earthly systems, ideologies, and territories, seeking to maintain spiritual darkness.

We also see evidence of **demonic strongholds in cities** throughout Scripture. Jesus frequently confronted demons in specific towns (e.g., Capernaum, Gadara), and the early church witnessed widespread demonic activity in bustling cities like Ephesus (Acts 19). This implies that cities and regions can indeed fall under prevailing spiritual influences, manifesting as specific patterns of sin, idolatry, or resistance to God's truth.

How Territorial Spirits Operate: These powerful entities are not passive observers; they actively work to maintain their dominion. They subtly and overtly:

- **Influence Culture and Ideologies:** These spirits weave ungodly belief systems, moral decay, idolatry, and anti-God philosophies into the very fabric of society within their assigned regions. They promote narratives that contradict God's truth, shaping public opinion and societal norms.

- **Hinder the Gospel:** They strategically resist the spread of the Good News, creating spiritual blindness and fostering opposition to genuine revival and evangelism (2 Corinthians 4:4). They aim to keep people from hearing and responding to the truth.

- **Foster Division and Conflict:** They sow seeds of discord, strife, violence, and hatred within communities and nations, preventing unity, peace, and cooperation. This can manifest in political unrest, social unrest, or even ethnic conflicts.

- **Maintain Strongholds:** These spirits entrench specific sins or mindsets, such as poverty, violence, sexual perversion, witchcraft, religious deception, or apathy, to keep regions bound. They establish a "spiritual atmosphere" that makes it difficult for people to break free.

Storming the Gates: Breaking Corporate Strongholds

Just as individuals can be held captive by spiritual strongholds (2 Corinthians 10:4–5), so too can entire communities, institutions, and even nations. These corporate strongholds manifest as entrenched patterns of evil, injustice, or spiritual darkness that seem to defy natural solutions. Breaking them requires a unified, strategic, and Spirit-led approach by the Body of Christ.

Identifying the Stronghold: Uncovering the Enemy's Strategy The journey to breaking corporate strongholds begins with deep, corporate prayer, fasting, and spiritual discernment. Seek the Holy Spirit's revelation: What are the dominant spiritual influences, the prevailing sins, or the anti-God attitudes that characterize this area?

- **Historical Research:** Understanding the history of the area is crucial. Were there past occult activities, ungodly covenants, significant bloodshed, racial injustice, deep-seated corruption, or widespread idolatry that may have given place to corporate bondage? This "spiritual mapping"—identifying the spiritual history and condition of an area—is often crucial to understand the enemy's "legal ground."

- **Mapping Spiritual Terrain:** This might involve prayer walks through significant sites (e.g., former slave markets, sites of mass violence, centers of witchcraft, government buildings, financial districts) to pray, repent on behalf of the land, and prophetically reclaim them for God's purposes. This physical engagement with spiritual intention can be powerful.

Strategies for Corporate Spiritual Warfare: United for Breakthrough Once the strongholds are identified, the Body of Christ can engage in strategic warfare:

- **Unified Prayer and Fasting:** This is the most potent weapon in corporate warfare (Joel 2:12-17; Acts 13:2-3). When believers unite with a common vision in sustained prayer and fasting, it creates a powerful spiritual force that can break demonic resistance and shift spiritual atmospheres over a region. Corporate spiritual engagement activates divine intervention.

- **Repentance for Corporate Sin:** Just as personal repentance is vital, believers can corporately repent on behalf of their community or nation for historical and present sins that have given the enemy legal ground (Nehemiah 1:4–11; Daniel 9:3-20). This act of humility and identification can release God's mercy and restoration over a land.

- **Declarations and Proclamations:** As Ezekiel prophesied to dry bones, speaking life into them (Ezekiel 37:4-10), we can prophetically declare

God's promises and sovereignty over our cities and regions. This involves renouncing darkness and proclaiming revival, truth, and righteousness over the territorial spirits.

- **Praise and Worship:** Corporate praise and worship are powerful spiritual weapons that can dismantle enemy strongholds. As demonstrated in 2 Chronicles 20, when the people praised, God set ambushes against their enemies. Worship invites God's manifest presence and paralyzes the enemy, shifting the spiritual atmosphere.

- **Acts of Righteousness and Justice:** Engaging actively in social justice initiatives, mercy ministries, and practical acts of righteousness within the community can dismantle the works of darkness in tangible ways (Isaiah 58:6-12). When the church actively cares for the poor, fights injustice, and brings light to dark places, yokes are broken, and ruins are rebuilt, demonstrating the Kingdom of God.

- **Targeted Intercession:** Intercessors can specifically address identified strongholds.

Rebuke spirits assigned to the area (e.g., spirit of witchcraft, pride, perversion, racism, poverty), binding them and loosing God's truth, healing, and light into the region (Matthew 18:18).

Warriors on Their Knees: The Power of Intercessory Deliverance

You don't always need to be physically present or laying hands on someone to engage in their deliverance. Intercessory deliverance is the profound spiritual act of standing in the gap for someone else and engaging in warfare on their behalf, from a distance. It is a vital expression of love and spiritual warfare.

The Unseen Strength: The Power of Intercession

- **Standing in the Gap:** Like Moses interceding for Israel (Exodus 32:11-14) or Jesus interceding for Peter (Luke 22:32), intercessors bear the burdens of others and plead before God for their release. You become a conduit for God's liberating power to flow into another's life.

- **Aligning with God's Heart:** God's will is freedom for all (John 8:36). Persistent prayer aligns us perfectly with His compassionate heart and sovereign will, activating His power on behalf of the afflicted.

- **Operating in Spiritual Authority:** As believers, we are seated with Christ in heavenly places (Ephesians 2:6). We pray not as beggars but as ambassadors, exercising the spiritual authority Christ has delegated to us.

Engaging in Intercessory Deliverance: Practical Steps

- **Seek Discernment:** Begin by asking the Holy Spirit for discernment regarding the person's situation. Is there a demonic influence? What is its nature or "assignment"? This precision in prayer is key.

- **Repentance and Identification:** Where possible and led by the Spirit, confess general sins or ancestral iniquities that may have given the enemy legal ground (Daniel 9:3–20). This act of identification can clear the spiritual atmosphere for breakthrough.

- **Binding and Loosing (Matthew 18:18):** In prayer, actively bind the works of darkness and the specific demonic spirits operating in the person's life. Simultaneously, loose the peace, presence, truth, and light of God into their situation.

- **Spiritual Decrees and Commands:** Speak with authority: "In the name of Jesus, I command every spirit of oppression, fear, addiction, [name specific spirit] to loose this person now and go!" Speak life and freedom over them.

- **Pray for the Infilling of the Holy Spirit:** After commanding spirits to leave, always invite the Holy Spirit to take full residence where bondage has broken. Pray for them to be filled with God's peace, joy, and love. Pray in tongues if applicable, as it builds up your spirit (1 Corinthians 14:4).

- **Persistence in Prayer:** Deliverance can be progressive. Maintain regular, consistent intercession until breakthrough occurs, trusting God's timing and power.

- **Maintain Confidentiality:** Always pray with love and discretion. Guard people's privacy and dignity, sharing only what is necessary with trusted prayer partners.

The Grand Commission: Advancing the Kingdom

The call to spiritual warfare is not reserved for a select few—it is the mission of every believer. Jesus didn't just free individuals; He transformed cities. He overturned the systems of the enemy and established His Kingdom wherever He walked. Now, as His body, we continue that mission, carrying His light into every dark corner of the world.

Wherever darkness reigns—whether in a home, a school, a city hall, or an entire nation—we are called to be light (Matthew 5:14). As we mature in discernment and authority, let us take our place as watchmen, intercessors, and reformers. By understanding territorial warfare, confronting corporate strongholds, and practicing intercessory deliverance, we partner with Heaven to see regions restored and captives liberated. The ultimate victory is assured: "The kingdoms of this world have become the kingdoms of our Lord and of His Christ, and He shall reign forever and ever" (Revelation 11:15).

Sustaining Your Freedom: What Comes Next?

In the next chapter, we will confront the hidden roots that often perpetuate bondage—generational curses. We will explore how these curses gain legal ground, how to break them through Christ's redemptive work, and how to release generational blessings instead. This next step in your journey equips you to rewrite your family's spiritual legacy with the authority of Christ.

Application Moment: Take Ground for God

1. **Reflect:**
   Are you advancing the Kingdom in your family, community, or region—or just surviving spiritually?
   Have you taken your spiritual authority seriously?

2. **Repent:**
   "Lord, I've settled for survival. I repent for not standing in authority. I ask You to use me for Kingdom impact."

3. **Respond:**
   Pray over your neighborhood, city, or
   workplace. Declare freedom and blessing.
   Say aloud:
   *"I take spiritual ground in the name of Jesus.
   This territory belongs to God."*

Chapter 18

BREAKING CURSES AND RELEASING BLESSINGS

Deliverance is a profound liberation, but for freedom to be truly complete and deeply rooted, the lingering legal rights of darkness must be canceled, and the full inheritance of blessing must be received. Just as personal freedom must be maintained, so too must generational patterns of bondage be broken, and the power of spoken curses reversed. Scripture offers both the diagnosis and the divine prescription: curses can be broken, and blessings released—all through the finished, redemptive work of Jesus Christ on the cross.

> **"I have set before you life and death, blessings and curses. Now choose life [...]" —Deuteronomy 30:19**

The Invisible Threads: Understanding Curses and Blessings

Curses and blessings are far more than mere poetic language or ancient superstition. They are powerful spiritual **pronouncements**—verbal declarations that invoke spiritual consequence, setting in motion either good or ill. These effects can be activated by God Himself, by other people, by our own words, or by the enemy.

- A **blessing** is a spiritual declaration that imparts favor, fruitfulness, peace, and divine protection. It opens pathways for God's goodness to flow.

- A **curse** is a spiritual declaration that brings restriction, frustration, loss, and oppression. It aims to hinder, bind, and destroy.

Both blessings and curses can linger and manifest through **generations**, affecting not only individuals but also entire families, communities, and even nations. Just as blessings have "staying power" when covenant conditions are met (Deuteronomy 28:1-14), so do curses—especially when sin remains unrepented of, providing a "legal ground" for their continued operation.

> "The causeless curse does not alight."
> —Proverbs 26:2

This proverb is a crucial insight: a curse without a cause (an open door, a legal ground) will not land or take root. This means curses are not arbitrary; they operate according to spiritual laws, often linked to unconfessed sin, disobedience, or occult involvement.

Seeds of Sorrow: Where Curses Take Root

Curses are a recurring theme throughout Scripture, demonstrating their reality and impact. They can arise from multiple sources, each creating a unique point of vulnerability:

- **God-Initiated Curses:** These are divine judgments pronounced for specific violations of God's covenant and commands (e.g., Deuteronomy 27–28). They are a consequence of severe disobedience, such as idolatry, injustice, or sexual immorality. God's curses are righteous judgments against sin.

- **Human Pronouncements:** Words carry immense spiritual power (Proverbs 18:21). People may curse others through bitter words, gossip, slander, malicious soulish prayers, or even through a parent's angry outburst over a child (James 3:9–10; Proverbs 17:13). These can be spoken knowingly or unknowingly.

- **Authority Figures:** Those in positions of authority—parents, spiritual leaders, or even government figures—can speak curses (or blessings) that carry significant weight. For example, Jacob's unwitting curse on Rachel in Genesis 31:32 had tragic consequences.

- **Self-Imposed Curses:** These are surprisingly common and insidious. They occur when we speak negatively over ourselves, make foolish oaths, or repeatedly declare destructive beliefs about our identity or future (e.g., "I'll never succeed," "I'm always sick," "I'm so stupid"). The words we speak over ourselves can become self-fulfilling prophecies, inviting spiritual agreement from the enemy (Matthew 27:25).

- **Occult Involvement and Idolatry:** Engaging in occult practices or idolatry (as explored in Chapter 8) creates direct open doors for demonic influence and often activates generational curses. God strictly warns against these practices, as they invite judgment upon succeeding generations (Exodus 20:5; Deuteronomy 18:9–14).

- **Satanic Sources:** Curses spoken by witches, mediums, or under direct demonic influence may take hold when there is unconfessed sin or an existing vulnerability that provides a "legal ground" for the curse to alight.

Unmasking the Patterns: Recognizing a Curse's Mark

How can you tell if a curse might be operating in your life or family? While not every hardship is a curse, and discernment (Chapter 11) is key, certain persistent patterns can be strong indicators. The Holy Spirit will often highlight these recurring issues, revealing the spiritual root beneath the surface.

Common symptoms of a curse may include:

- **Chronic Illness or Mental Breakdown:** Persistent, unexplainable sicknesses, mental anguish, or recurring psychological disorders that defy medical or therapeutic solutions.

- **Repeated Miscarriages or Infertility:** A consistent pattern of barrenness or loss in a family line.

- **Cycles of Poverty or Failure:** A recurring inability to prosper financially, despite effort, or a pattern of repeated business failures.

- **Unnatural Deaths or Suicides:** A disturbing pattern of premature deaths, accidents, or suicides within a family line.

- **Consistent Relational Breakdown:** A history of broken marriages, dysfunctional family relationships, or an inability to maintain healthy connections.

- **Self-Hatred, Shame, or Destructive Addictions:** Deep-seated self-loathing, overwhelming shame, or compulsive addictions that seem impossible to break.

The most telling clues to a curse are **patterns persisting across generations** or the **repetition of negative**

events without a clear natural explanation. When you see the same destructive "fruit" appearing repeatedly in a family tree, it's a strong invitation to investigate the possibility of a generational curse.

The Cross: Our Ultimate Curse-Breaker

The good news, the glorious truth of the Gospel, is that Jesus Christ became the curse on our behalf. On the cross, He bore the full penalty of the Law and utterly dismantled the authority of every curse that could ever be pronounced against us.

> **"Christ redeemed us from the curse of the law by becoming a curse for us, for it is written: 'Cursed is everyone who is hung on a pole.'" —Galatians 3:13**

In Christ, a **divine exchange** occurs: our curses are absorbed by Him, and His blessings are released upon us. He took our judgment so we could receive His favor. But just like Israel had to *act* on their inheritance to possess the Promised Land, we too must **act on our inheritance** of freedom through confession, repentance, and spiritual warfare to see curses broken and blessings released in our lives.

Stepping into Liberty: Practical Steps to Break Curses

Breaking a curse is an act of faith and authority, applying the finished work of Christ to your specific situation. Here are **seven practical, scriptural steps** to walk out your freedom:

1. **Establish a Scriptural Foundation:** Begin by firmly rooting yourself in the truth of your authority in Christ. Understand that through Him, you have power over all the power of the enemy (Luke 10:19; Colossians 1:13–14; Ephesians 1:7). You are no longer under the domain of darkness.

2. **Confess Faith in Christ:** Humbly acknowledge Jesus as your Lord and Savior (Romans 10:10). This personal declaration of faith is the foundation of your right to freedom.

3. **Commit to Obedience:** Choose to walk in righteousness and obedience to God's Word (1 Samuel 15:22). This closes any new doors to the enemy and strengthens your spiritual position.

4. **Confess Personal and Ancestral Sin:** Bring any

known sins—yours or those of your ancestors—under the cleansing blood of Jesus (Leviticus 26:40; Proverbs 28:13). Identify with the sins of your family line that may have given the curse legal ground, and repent on their behalf.

5. **Forgive Others and Yourself:** Unforgiveness is a powerful spiritual chain that holds curses in place (Matthew 18:34–35). Release those who have hurt you, and release yourself from any self-condemnation (Mark 11:25–26). This act of forgiveness dismantles the enemy's legal right to torment.

6. **Renounce Occult and Ungodly Activity:** Verbally reject and sever all contact with the occult, idolatry, false covenants, and any ungodly practices (Acts 19:18–19; Deuteronomy 7:25–26). This is a crucial step in removing any remaining "legal ground."

7. **Break the Curse in Jesus' Name:** With spiritual authority, declare the curse broken over your life and bloodline. Speak it aloud! Then, simultaneously, release the blessing of Christ,

purchased by His blood, over yourself and your family (James 4:7; Matthew 18:18).

Prayer of Release (Self-Ministered) This prayer can serve as a powerful template for breaking curses over your life. Speak it with conviction and faith:

"Lord Jesus Christ, I believe You are the Son of God and the only way to the Father. I confess my sins and the sins of my ancestors. I ask for Your forgiveness and cleansing by Your precious blood. I renounce all contact with occult practices, false religion, idolatry, and every form of sin that has opened doors to curses in my life or my family line. I forgive everyone who has ever harmed me, and I release them now from my heart. In Your mighty name, Jesus, I break every curse spoken over me or operating in my bloodline. I cancel all legal rights of the enemy, and I declare that I am redeemed from the curse of the law. I receive the blessing of Abraham and the fullness of Your blessing, purchased by Your blood. Fill me with Your Holy Spirit, and help me to walk in complete freedom and righteousness from this day forward. Amen."

Securing Your Inheritance: Sealing the Breakthrough

Breaking a curse is a powerful moment, but like any deliverance, it must be followed by intentional steps to seal the breakthrough and prevent re-entry.

- **Dedicate Your Life and Household to Christ:** Make a conscious decision to surrender every area of your life and your home to the Lordship of Jesus Christ. This creates a spiritual boundary and a holy dwelling place for God's presence.

- **Destroy Physical Items Linked to Sin or Occultism:** Following the example of Acts 19:19, physically destroy any objects, books, or items that were used in or represent past sin, occult involvement, or idolatry. This is a tangible act of severing ties.

- **Anoint Your Home and Speak Blessing Aloud:** Spiritually cleanse your living space.

253

You can anoint your home with oil (a biblical symbol of consecration) and speak blessings aloud over it, inviting God's presence and protection (Numbers 6:24–26).

- **Replace Lies with Truth:** Actively replace the lies and negative declarations associated with the broken curse with God's truth through daily Scripture declarations and meditation (Romans 12:2). This renews your mind and reinforces your new identity in Christ.

The Final Commission: Walking in Fullness

With curses broken and blessings released, you're positioned for sustained freedom and fruitful living. This is not just a personal journey—it's a commission to set captives free in Jesus' name. You are now equipped to rewrite your family's spiritual legacy with the authority of Christ, becoming a channel of blessing for generations to come.

Application Moment: Break the Old, Release the New

1. **Reflect:**
   Do you notice repeated struggles or patterns in your family line? *Have you ever spoken blessings over your own life or family to replace old curses?*

2. **Repent:**
   "I renounce every generational curse—spoken or lived. I choose the blessing of God."

3. **Respond:**
   Write down a curse (e.g., "anger," "poverty," "abandonment") and speak a blessing to replace it (e.g., "peace," "provision," "faithfulness").
   Declare:
   "I am not cursed—I am blessed. I receive the full inheritance of freedom in Christ."

HOW TO USE THIS STUDY GUIDE

This guide is a companion to *Whom the Son Sets Free*, crafted to lead individuals and small groups through the principles of spiritual freedom, emotional healing, and deliverance. Whether used in a church setting, a discipleship group, or a personal ministry team, these sessions are designed to be Spirit-led, safe, and transformative.

Group Structure and Rhythm

- **Group Size:** 3 to 8 participants is optimal for meaningful interaction and personal prayer.
- **Schedule:** Weekly meetings of 60–90 minutes work well. Adjust as led by the Holy Spirit.
- **Materials:** Each person should have this book, a Bible, a journal, and a teachable spirit.

Leader Guidance

- **Lead with Grace:** Create an atmosphere of compassion, confidentiality, and non-judgment.
- **Rely on the Holy Spirit:** Stay flexible. Let the Spirit lead beyond scripted moments.
- **Model Vulnerability:** Your transparency as a leader sets the tone for others to be real.

- **Discern Carefully:** Not all healing is immediate—be prayerful and discerning in deliverance moments.

Session Flow

Each session may include:

1. **Opening Prayer** – Welcome the presence of the Holy Spirit and surrender the time.
2. **Scripture Focus** – Anchor the session in the Word.
3. **Teaching Review** – Summarize key points from the assigned chapter.
4. **Discussion Questions** – Engage the group with reflective, heart-level prompts.
5. **Prayer and Ministry Time** – Allow space for the Holy Spirit to bring healing or revelation.
6. **Weekly Reflection** – Optional journaling or prayer prompts for personal growth.

When Ministering Deliverance

If your group is engaging in personal deliverance or renunciation:

- **Never minister alone.** Always pray in pairs or with team members.
- **Maintain safety and order.** This is not a performance—it is a holy process.
- **Use the tools provided.** Refer to the renunciation prayers, declarations, and checklists in the appendices.

"Now the Lord is the Spirit, and where the Spirit of the Lord is, there is freedom."
—2 Corinthians 3:17

APPENDIX A: SPEAKING LIFE AND BREAKING CHAINS

DELIVERANCE PRAYERS & DECLARATIONS

Purpose: This appendix is designed to equip you with biblically grounded, Spirit-led prayer tools to walk in personal deliverance, minister to others, and affirm your identity in Christ. These resources are not magical formulas, but powerful expressions of faith and authority, designed to align your heart and words with God's will for freedom. In the spiritual realm, words carry immense power (Proverbs 18:21). When spoken aloud in faith, rooted in Scripture, and empowered by the Holy Spirit, these prayers and declarations become potent weapons in spiritual warfare, tools for inner healing, and catalysts for renewal. Speak them with conviction, expecting the tangible presence and power of the Holy Spirit to respond.

Prayers for Breakthrough: Engaging the Deliverer

These prayers are designed to guide you in specific acts of spiritual warfare, addressing common areas of bondage and inviting the liberating power of Jesus Christ.

A Personal Cry for Freedom: The Self-Deliverance Prayer This prayer is a powerful tool for individual use, allowing you to actively engage in breaking cycles of bondage over your own life. Approach it with a humble heart, radical honesty, and firm faith in Jesus' supreme authority. It covers confession, renunciation, and commanding spirits to leave, inviting the Holy Spirit to fill the cleansed space.

"Lord Jesus, I acknowledge You as my Savior, Deliverer, and Lord. (Romans 10:9) I confess all my sins—both known and unknown—and I repent of them now. (1 John 1:9) I renounce every agreement, conscious or unconscious, I have made with darkness, including ungodly beliefs, negative self-talk, or any participation in practices that do not honor You. (Acts 19:18-19) I plead the precious blood of Jesus over my life, my mind, my emotions, and my body—for cleansing, protection, and liberation. (Revelation 12:11; Hebrews 9:14) In Your mighty name, I command every spirit of fear, torment, anxiety, shame, guilt, addiction, infirmity, and any other oppressive spirit to leave me now and never return. (Mark 16:17; Luke 10:19) I declare that I am free, healed, and made whole by Your finished work on the cross. (Galatians 5:1; Isaiah 53:5) I receive Your freedom, peace, and healing by faith, and I surrender every area of my life to Your Lordship. Amen." (James 4:7)

Rewriting the Legacy: Prayer for Family Deliverance This prayer focuses on breaking generational patterns and demonic assignments that may have affected your family line. You are standing in the gap for your lineage, declaring a new spiritual inheritance in Christ, rooted in His redemptive work.

"Father, I lift up my family to You—both immediate and extended. I stand in the gap for them and confess the sins of my ancestors and any ungodly patterns, idolatry, or occult involvement that have afflicted our lineage. (Leviticus 26:40; Exodus 20:5) I repent on behalf of my family. In the name of Jesus, I break every generational curse and every demonic assignment operating through our bloodline. (Galatians 3:13) I declare that the cycle of bondage is broken by the blood of Jesus. (Revelation 12:11) Let every unclean spirit, every stronghold of darkness, and every ungodly influence be uprooted and cast out of our family lineage. I sever every ungodly soul tie that connects family members to past wounds, sinful patterns, or spiritual oppression. I speak healing, reconciliation, unity, and righteousness over our household. (Ephesians 4:32) Let Your light expose all darkness, and Your love prevail. (John 1:5) In Jesus' name, I declare my family is set free and consecrated to You. Amen." (Joshua 24:15)

Severing Unhealthy Connections: Breaking Ungodly Soul Ties Soul ties are deep emotional or spiritual bonds formed through intense relationships.[12] While some are godly (like marriage), ungodly soul ties can create unhealthy dependencies or allow spiritual influence (1 Corinthians 6:16-17). This prayer focuses on severing those unhealthy connections that hinder your freedom and draw you away from Christ.

"In the name of Jesus Christ, I acknowledge and confess any ungodly soul ties I have formed—whether through sexual sin, emotional manipulation, control, idolatry, or other unholy alliances. (1 John 1:9) I repent for my participation in these connections. I now consciously and decisively break every such ungodly soul tie, severing the spiritual and emotional connection. (2 Corinthians 10:4-5) I renounce any claim or legal right these ties have given to demonic spirits. (Ephesians 4:27) I command every spirit associated with these ungodly soul ties to go now, completely and permanently. I declare that I am whole, complete, and free in Christ Jesus. (Colossians 2:10) My affections

---

[12] **Soul ties** refer to the deep emotional, psychological, and spiritual bonds formed between individuals. While the term itself is not explicitly found in Scripture, the concept is derived from biblical examples such as David and Jonathan (1 Samuel 18:1), sexual union (Genesis 2:24; 1 Corinthians 6:16), and unhealthy relational attachments (Judges 16:4–21; Proverbs 6:26). Soul ties can be **godly**, fostering covenant and unity, or **ungodly**, forming through sexual sin, emotional manipulation, trauma bonding, or idolatrous relationships. These ties can influence behavior, emotions, and spiritual openness, often requiring intentional prayer and severance for freedom. Brown, Rebecca. *Prepare for War.* New Kensington, PA: Whitaker House, 1987. See also: Anderson, Neil T. *The Bondage Breaker.* Eugene, OR: Harvest House, 1990.

and loyalties belong to Christ alone. Amen." (Matthew 22:37)

Shutting the Gates: Closing Occult Doors If you or your ancestors have had any involvement with occult practices, false religions, or spiritism, this prayer is vital to close those spiritual doors and remove any legal ground the enemy may claim (Deuteronomy 18:9-12). This is a decisive act of turning away from darkness and declaring sole allegiance to God.

"Heavenly Father, I humbly come before You, repenting for any and all involvement—direct or indirect—with the occult, witchcraft, divination, sorcery, false religion, New Age practices, spiritism, idolatry, or any activity that opens doors to demonic influence. (Acts 19:18-19) I renounce every oath, vow, dedication, or agreement made knowingly or unknowingly with darkness. I break every curse, hex, spell, or assignment sent against me through these practices. (Galatians 3:13) I declare that the blood of Jesus nullifies and destroys every legal right the enemy has used against me or my family due to these involvements. (Colossians 2:14-15) I proclaim that Jesus Christ is Lord over every area of my life—past, present, and future. (Philippians 2:9-11) I close every door to the enemy and invite the Holy Spirit to fill every space once yielded to darkness. Amen." (Ephesians 5:18)

Breaking Generational Chains: A Comprehensive Prayer This prayer focuses specifically on dismantling generational curses and patterns, applying the full redemptive power of Christ to your lineage. It's a powerful declaration of a new spiritual inheritance.

"Father God, in the name of Jesus, I come before You and acknowledge any generational sins, curses, or iniquities passed down through my family bloodline. (Leviticus 26:40) I repent for the sins of my ancestors and for any agreements—spoken or unspoken—that have allowed these patterns to continue. (Daniel 9:3-20) By the authority of Jesus Christ and the power of His blood, I break and renounce every generational curse operating in my life and family. (Galatians 3:13; Revelation 12:11) I sever every demonic assignment tied to these curses—whether of sickness, poverty, divorce, addiction, fear, rebellion, or perversion. I declare that these patterns are broken, nullified, and powerless over me and my descendants. I speak blessing, favor, healing, and restoration over my lineage from this day forward. (Deuteronomy 30:19) Thank You, Lord, that I am grafted into the family of God and that the blood of Jesus rewrites my generational story. (Romans 11:17) I receive freedom and declare that my household shall serve the Lord. Amen." (Joshua 24:15)

The Full Armor of God: A Comprehensive Deliverance Prayer Adapted from Joy Lamb's *The Sword of the Spirit, The Word of God*, this prayer is a comprehensive approach to spiritual warfare, covering various areas of influence and affirming God's sovereignty.

"In the name of the Lord Jesus Christ, and by the power of His blood and the Holy Spirit, I lift to the Lord myself, my family, home, neighborhood, church, workplace, city, state, nation, and the world, and each person and area for whom I am praying. (Ephesians 6:18) I plead the blood of Jesus Christ over all of us for our protection. (Revelation 12:11) Whatsoever is bound on earth is bound in heaven; whatsoever is loosed on earth is loosed in heaven (Matthew 16:19). I bind satan, the spirits, powers, and forces of darkness. I bind any demonic assignments sent against any of the people and areas I am lifting up. (Ephesians 6:12) I bind all interaction and communication of spirits and command them in Jesus' name to go to His feet. I loose the Holy Spirit and holy angels to cleanse and fill each place previously affected by darkness with the love and life of Christ. (Galatians 5:22-23; Hebrews 1:14) I break all curses, hexes, spells, and demonic activity—past and present—over myself and those I intercede for. (Colossians 2:14-15) I renounce and ask forgiveness for all negative inner vows and command all generational bondages, weaknesses, and disorders to be cut off. (Numbers 30:2; Isaiah 10:27) I place the Cross of Jesus between every ungodly relationship and declare: We are cut free and free indeed (John 8:36). I claim the blood of Jesus over all I've lifted to You, Lord. In Jesus' name. Amen."

II. Declarations for Identity & Freedom: Speaking Truth Over Your Life

Regularly declaring biblical truths aloud is a powerful practice that reinforces your identity in Christ and builds spiritual strength, creating a shield against the enemy's lies (Proverbs 18:21). These are your spiritual truths, rooted in Scripture, affirming your authority, identity, and freedom in Christ. Speak them with conviction daily, allowing them to transform your mindset and establish God's reality in your life.

- I am a new creation in Christ; old things have passed away, behold, all things have become new. (2 Corinthians 5:17)
- I have been given authority to trample on serpents and scorpions, and over all the power of the enemy, and nothing shall by any means hurt me. (Luke 10:19)
- I am sealed with the Holy Spirit and belong to God; I am God's treasured possession. (Ephesians 1:13-14)
- No weapon formed against me shall prosper, and every tongue which rises against me in judgment I shall condemn. This is my heritage as a servant of the Lord. (Isaiah 54:17)

- I am fearfully and wonderfully made by God. (Psalm 139:14)
- I am more than a conqueror through Him who loved me. (Romans 8:37)
- I am redeemed from the curse of the law, for Christ became a curse for me. (Galatians 3:13)
- I am the righteousness of God in Christ Jesus. (2 Corinthians 5:21)
- I am blood-washed and blood-bought; I overcome by the blood of the Lamb and the word of my testimony. (1 John 1:7; Revelation 12:11)
- I renounce every ungodly soul tie and declare myself free from all unhealthy connections. (1 Corinthians 6:16)
- I am free from every generational curse, sickness, and disease, for by His stripes I am healed. (1 Peter 2:24)
- I walk by faith, not by sight, trusting in God's unseen realities. (2 Corinthians 5:7)
- I am free from pride, lust, perversion, rebellion, witchcraft, idolatry, poverty, rejection, fear, confusion, addiction, death, and destruction—in the name of Jesus.
- I am free from financial curses from my ancestors—in the name of Jesus.
- I command inherited sickness and disease to leave my body—in the name of Jesus.
- I am free from all generational, racial, gender, and geographic traumas, for God is doing a new thing; now it springs forth! (Isaiah 43:18–19)

APPENDIX B: DIAGNOSTIC & PREPARATORY TOOLS FOR FREEDOM

Purpose: This section provides diagnostic and practical tools to help individuals and ministry leaders identify areas of spiritual oppression, prepare for personal or group deliverance, and facilitate lasting inner healing. These tools support prayerful self-assessment and intentional freedom work under the guidance of the Holy Spirit, ensuring a more targeted and effective approach to liberation.

Diagnostic Checklist: Am I Under Oppression?

Instructions: Prayerfully review each question and answer honestly. This checklist is designed to help you identify potential areas where demonic oppression or strongholds might be present. It is a tool for self-discernment, not a definitive diagnosis. Be transparent with yourself and with God as you mark each with ☑ (Yes) or ✖ (No).

- Do you struggle with intrusive, tormenting thoughts (e.g., thoughts of self-harm, constant negativity, blasphemous thoughts, fear-inducing scenarios) that feel alien or difficult to control (2 Corinthians 10:5)?

- Have you experienced persistent nightmares, night terrors, or sleep paralysis (feeling awake but unable to move, often accompanied by a sense of evil presence) (Mark 9:26)?
- Are you trapped in cycles of addiction or compulsive behavior (e.g., pornography, substance abuse, excessive gaming, anger outbursts, overeating) that you desperately want to stop but feel powerless to overcome (Romans 7:15-20)?
- Do you experience sudden, unexplainable emotional shifts (e.g., rapid swings from peace to intense anger, deep sadness, or anxiety without a clear trigger) (James 1:8)?
- Do you sense a strong resistance or spiritual blockade when trying to pray or read the Bible, finding it difficult to focus, feeling sleepy, or experiencing distracting thoughts (2 Corinthians 4:4)?
- Have you knowingly or unknowingly participated in occult practices, New Age spirituality, visited psychics, used Ouija boards, or engaged in spiritual rituals outside of Christ (Deuteronomy 18:10-12)?
- Do you carry deep-seated unforgiveness, unresolved trauma, or chronic resentment towards yourself or others that seems to hinder your peace and relationships (Matthew 18:34-35)?

- Do you suffer from undiagnosed or persistent physical ailments or pain that doctors cannot diagnose or treat effectively (Luke 13:11)?
- Do you struggle with a profound sense of rejection, abandonment, worthlessness, or self-hatred that significantly impacts your self-perception and relationships (Psalm 27:10)?
- Do you frequently feel a sense of spiritual heaviness, dread, or a dark, oppressive presence around you or in your home (Isaiah 61:3)?

Scoring Guide: Interpreting Your Results

This guide provides general recommendations based on your responses. Remember, this is a guide, and the Holy Spirit's leading is always paramount.

- **1–2 "Yes" Responses: Low Risk**
  - **Recommendation:** Continue to pursue ongoing discipleship, regular prayer, and consistent Bible study. These may be common spiritual struggles that can be overcome through consistent spiritual practices and growth in Christ (Ephesians 4:22-24).
- **3–5 "Yes" Responses: Moderate Risk**
  - **Recommendation:** These indicate potential areas of spiritual oppression or strongholds. It's advisable to seek counsel from a trusted pastor, spiritual mentor, or

mature Christian leader. Prayerfully consider engaging in focused deliverance prayers and potentially inner healing sessions to address these areas (James 5:16).

- **6+ "Yes" Responses: High Risk**
  - ○ **Recommendation:** This indicates a significant likelihood of demonic oppression or deeply entrenched strongholds. It is strongly recommended that you urgently seek guidance and a formal deliverance session with an experienced, biblically sound ministry team. Commit to comprehensive inner healing work to address root causes and fortify your spiritual well-being (Mark 16:17).

Preparing for Freedom: Essential Questions for Reflection

These questions are designed to help you prepare your heart and mind for a deliverance session or deeper healing ministry event. Honest reflection on these areas will help the Holy Spirit reveal specific roots of bondage and prepare you for breakthrough. Write your responses in a journal or be prepared to share them with a trusted ministry leader.

- Are there any recurring sins or patterns in your life that you desperately want to break but feel powerless to overcome (Romans 7:15-20)?
- Are you aware of any trauma, abuse, or betrayal from your past that remains unresolved, causing you emotional pain or affecting your relationships (Psalm 147:3)?
- Have you ever practiced or participated in occult, witchcraft, New Age, or non-Christian spiritual rituals, even if unknowingly or out of curiosity (Deuteronomy 18:9-12)?
- Do you sense any ungodly soul ties or emotionally unhealthy attachments to individuals (past or present) that drain your spiritual energy or hinder your freedom (1 Corinthians 6:16-17)?
- Are you holding on to unforgiveness toward anyone—including yourself—for past hurts or offenses (Matthew 6:14-15)?
- Have you made any inner vows or ungodly agreements with yourself or others (e.g., "I'll never trust anyone," "I'll always be alone") (Numbers 30:2)?
- Is there any known generational sin or curse in your family line that you believe might be affecting you (Exodus 20:5)?

III. Activating Freedom: Practical Tools for Renunciation & Ministry

These tools provide clear, actionable steps for both personal engagement and for ministers facilitating deliverance.

A. The Renunciation Worksheet: Breaking Specific Strongholds Use this format to verbally renounce and break specific strongholds, lies, or past involvements. This is a powerful act of your will, severing ties with darkness.

"In the name of Jesus Christ, I renounce [insert specific sin, trauma, spirit, or involvement, e.g., 'the spirit of fear,' 'the lie that I am worthless,' 'my past involvement with tarot cards']. (Acts 19:18-19) I break every agreement I have made—knowingly or unknowingly—with this spirit or stronghold. (2 Corinthians 10:4-5) I apply the blood of Jesus over this area of my life and declare I am free and cleansed. (Revelation 12:11) I command all spirits connected to [name the issue] to leave me now and never return. (Mark 16:17) I surrender this area completely to the Lordship of Jesus and receive His healing and truth. Amen." (James 4:7)

B. Deliverance Session Summary: A Ministry Blueprint This outlines the basic steps for ministers conducting a deliverance session, ensuring a structured and effective approach.

- **Repentance:** Lead the individual in specific confession and repentance for known sins (1 John 1:9). This clears the legal ground.
- **Renunciation:** Guide the individual to verbally renounce all ties, spirits, and ungodly agreements (Acts 19:18-19).
- **Command:** Take authority in Jesus' name and command specific spirits to leave (Mark 16:17).
- **Replace:** Immediately invite the Holy Spirit to fill every cleansed space with His presence, peace, and truth (Ephesians 5:18; Matthew 12:43-45).
- **Sealing Prayer:** Conclude with a prayer declaring the person sealed by the blood of Jesus (Ephesians 1:13) and walking in sustained freedom and new identity.

C. Freedom Maintenance Practices: Living in Liberty After deliverance, encouraging these regular disciplines is crucial for maintaining newfound freedom and preventing re-entry. This is about building a lifestyle of liberty.

- **Daily Prayer and Scripture Reading:** Consistent communion with God and immersion in His Word are vital for spiritual strength and discernment (Psalm 119:105; Ephesians 6:18).
- **Speaking Identity Declarations:** Regularly declare truths about your identity and authority in Christ (see Appendix A) to reinforce your new

reality and counter the enemy's lies (Proverbs 18:21).

- **Staying Connected to a Bible-Believing Church:** Consistent fellowship, accountability, and spiritual covering within the Body of Christ are essential for sustained freedom (Hebrews 10:25).
- **Confessing Sin Quickly and Forgiving Continually:** Maintain short accounts with God and others to prevent new "legal grounds" from forming (1 John 1:9; Matthew 6:14-15).
- **Avoiding Triggering Environments or Media:** Be intentional about avoiding places, relationships, or media that previously led to sin or bondage (Proverbs 4:23).
- **Listening to Worship and Eliminating Occult Objects/Media from Home:** Create a spiritual atmosphere of praise and holiness in your home by playing worship music and actively removing any defiled objects or ungodly media (Joshua 24:15; Acts 19:19).

APPENDIX C: GROUP MINISTRY RESOURCES

Purpose: This section equips facilitators and ministry teams with practical guidance for leading safe, Spirit-filled group sessions focused on deliverance and inner healing. Whether you are working with a small discipleship group, a church ministry, or an intercession team, these tools will help foster an atmosphere of trust, safety, and transformative encounters with God. They provide a blueprint for creating environments where individuals can courageously pursue freedom in community.

Navigating Together: How to Use This Study Guide in a Group Setting

This book is designed not just for individual reading, but for shared exploration. Refer to the "How to Use This Study Guide" section (typically found near the Introduction of the main manuscript) for complete group structure and foundational principles. Here are some key reminders for facilitators:

- **Keep Group Size Manageable:** An ideal group size is typically 3–8 people. This allows for genuine connection, vulnerability, and sufficient time for each person to share and receive ministry. Larger groups may benefit from breaking into smaller discussion pods.

- **Essential Tools for Each Member:** Encourage every group member to bring their copy of this book, a Bible, a personal journal, and a willingness to engage in prayer and reflection.
- **Time Management:** Allocate 60–90 minutes for each meeting, adjusting as needed based on the depth of discussion and ministry time. Be mindful of the clock to honor everyone's time.
- **Opening and Closing with Prayer:** Always begin and end each session with prayer, inviting the Holy Spirit to lead, protect, and minister to each individual (John 14:26; Ephesians 6:18).
- **Creating a Safe Space:** Foster an atmosphere of absolute honesty, strict confidentiality, and compassionate ministry. Reassure members that what is shared in the group stays in the group, building trust and psychological safety.

The Rhythm of Freedom: Sample Weekly Session Format

This suggested flow provides a flexible structure for your group gatherings, ensuring a balanced approach to teaching, discussion, reflection, and ministry.

- **Welcome & Opening Prayer (5-10 minutes):** Begin with a warm welcome, icebreaker (optional), and an opening prayer. Invite the

Holy Spirit to lead the session, to bring revelation, and to minister to each heart.

- **Scripture Reading (5 minutes):** Anchor the session in God's Word by reading key verses related to the week's chapter. This sets a spiritual foundation for the discussion.

- **Teaching Summary (10-15 minutes):** Briefly recap the chapter's main themes and key takeaways. This helps refresh everyone's memory and ensures a shared understanding before discussion. You may use a short video or a prepared summary.

- **Discussion Questions (20-30 minutes):** Facilitate open discussion using the prepared prompts from the "Interactive Questions" section (Appendix B) or allow for spontaneous, Spirit-led dialogue. Encourage everyone to participate, but respect those who prefer to listen.

- **Personal Reflection & Listening Prayer (5–10 minutes):** Provide a quiet space for individual reflection. Encourage journaling, silent meditation on a Scripture, or simply listening for the Holy Spirit's voice regarding what was discussed. This allows for personal processing.

- **Ministry & Prayer Time (15-25 minutes):** This is the heart of the group ministry. Allow space for personal prayer requests, renunciation (as guided in Chapter 10), or deliverance as needed. Ministers can pray individually with group members, always in pairs (Ecclesiastes 4:9-12).

Be sensitive to the Holy Spirit's leading for specific ministry.

- **Closing Prayer (5 minutes):** Conclude with a powerful closing prayer. Declare identity, healing, and continued freedom over each person. Speak blessings over the group and their week ahead.

Guiding with Grace: Group Leader Guidelines

Leading a group focused on deliverance and inner healing requires both spiritual authority and profound humility. These guidelines will help you facilitate a safe, effective, and Spirit-led environment.

- **Lead with Humility and Dependence:** Remember you are a facilitator, not a "fixer." Your role is to create space for the Holy Spirit to minister. Remain humble, acknowledging that it is Christ who delivers (John 8:36), not your own strength or technique.
- **Stay Prayerful and Spirit-Led:** Don't rush ministry moments. Be sensitive to the Holy Spirit's leading, allowing Him to set the pace and direction of the session. Sometimes, silence is the most powerful ministry.
- **Ensure Safety and Integrity:** Avoid emotional pressure, manipulation, or sensationalism. The focus is on genuine freedom, not outward

display. Protect vulnerable individuals from any form of exploitation or judgment.

- **Maintain Strict Confidentiality:** What is shared in the group stays in the group. Reiterate this policy at the beginning of every session to build trust and encourage vulnerability (Proverbs 11:13).

- **Encourage Participation, Not Perfection:** Honor each person's pace and process. Some may be ready to share deeply, others may need more time. Celebrate small steps of obedience and breakthrough.

- **Know Your Limits:** Be aware of your own capacity and training. If complex trauma or severe mental health issues surface, be prepared to offer referrals to licensed Christian counselors or other qualified professionals (Proverbs 11:14).

Teamwork in the Spirit: Ministry Team Roles

For larger sessions or church-based deliverance groups, defining roles within the ministry team ensures order, effectiveness, and comprehensive care.

- **Lead Facilitator:** This individual sets the overall tone, guides the session flow, introduces topics, and coordinates the various ministry components. They are responsible for maintaining order and spiritual direction.

- **Intercessor(s):** These team members pray silently and fervently throughout the session, discerning spiritual activity, interceding for individuals, and supporting the ministers through prayer. Their role is vital in the unseen realm.
- **Ministry Partner(s):** These individuals pray alongside group members as needed, offering personal prayer, leading in renunciations, and ministering deliverance under the guidance of the Holy Spirit and the Lead Facilitator.
- **Admin/Note-Taker (Optional):** This role assists with practical logistics, such as managing sign-ups, distributing resources, and taking discreet, confidential notes for follow-up purposes.
- **Crucial Team Principle:** Always minister in pairs when laying hands on individuals or leading in personal prayer. This provides accountability, mutual discernment, and protection for both the minister and the recipient (Ecclesiastes 4:9-12).

Protecting the Vulnerable: Confidentiality & Care Policy

Establishing and upholding a clear confidentiality and care policy is paramount to protect each group member, build trust, and preserve the unity and integrity of the ministry.

- **Strict Confidentiality:** Emphasize and enforce that all testimonies, personal details, and confessions shared within the group are strictly confidential and are not to be discussed outside the group without explicit permission from the individual concerned.
- **Professional Referrals:** Be prepared to offer referrals to licensed Christian counselors, therapists, or other qualified professionals if trauma, severe mental health issues, or complex relational dynamics surface beyond the capacity or training of the ministry team. Deliverance ministry complements, but does not replace, professional care.
- **Respecting Personal Boundaries:** Allow space for silence or emotion. Never force anyone to speak, participate beyond their comfort level, or share details they are unwilling to disclose. Honor each person's pace and process.
- **Deliverance as a Process:** Remind all members that deliverance is often a process, not a one-time event. Encourage patience, persistence, and commitment to ongoing spiritual disciplines for sustained freedom.

Sparking Dialogue: Suggested Discussion Prompts

Use or adapt these prompts to facilitate rich group reflection and sharing each week. They are designed to encourage personal engagement with the chapter's themes.

- What truth or concept from this chapter stood out most to you and why? How did it resonate with your personal experience or current circumstances?
- Did you feel conviction, comfort, or clarity as you read this chapter? Can you describe any specific emotions or insights that arose?
- Have you ever experienced something similar to what the chapter described (e.g., a specific demonic tactic, a type of emotional wound, or a manifestation)? If comfortable, share briefly.
- What is God showing you about your identity in Christ, your past, or a specific area of your life through this chapter?
- Are there any areas you'd like to renounce, pray through, or bring into the light during our ministry time today?
- What questions or challenges remain for you after reading this chapter? What aspects would you like to explore further?
-

APPENDIX D: CATEGORIZED SCRIPTURE REFERENCE GUIDE

This guide provides biblical foundations for understanding and engaging in deliverance. Meditate on these Scriptures and allow them to build your faith.

Spiritual Authority

- **Luke 10:19:** "Behold, I give you the authority to trample on serpents and scorpions, and over all the power of the enemy, and nothing shall by any means hurt you." (Highlights the believer's delegated authority from Christ over demonic forces.)
- **Matthew 28:18–20:** "And Jesus came and spoke to them, saying, 'All authority has been given to Me in heaven and on earth. Go therefore and make disciples of all the nations, baptizing them in the name of the Father and of the Son and of the Holy Spirit, teaching them to observe all things that I have commanded you; and lo, I am with you always, even to the end of the age.' Amen." (Emphasizes Jesus' ultimate authority and His commission to believers to carry out His work.)

- **Mark 16:17–18:** "And these signs will follow those who believe: In My name they will cast out demons; they will speak with new tongues; they will take up serpents; and if they drink anything deadly, it will by no means hurt them; they will lay hands on the sick, and they will recover." (Confirms casting out demons as a sign that accompanies believers.)

Deliverance in Christ

- **Isaiah 61:1–2:** "The Spirit of the Lord GOD is upon Me, because the LORD has anointed Me to preach good tidings to the poor; He has sent Me to heal the brokenhearted, to proclaim liberty to the captives, and the opening of the prison to those who are bound; to proclaim the acceptable year of the LORD, and the day of vengeance of our God; to comfort all who mourn." (Prophecy fulfilled in Jesus, highlighting His ministry of liberation.)
- **John 8:36:** "Therefore if the Son makes you free, you shall be free indeed." (A foundational truth for deliverance, emphasizing true freedom found only in Christ.)
- **Colossians 1:13:** "He has delivered us from the power of darkness and conveyed us into the kingdom of the Son of His love." (Declares the believer's transfer from Satan's dominion to Christ's kingdom.)

Overcoming Fear

- **2 Timothy 1:7:** "For God has not given us a spirit of fear, but of power and of love and of a sound mind." (A direct declaration against the spirit of fear, emphasizing God's provision for believers.)
- **Psalm 27:1:** "The LORD is my light and my salvation; whom shall I fear? The LORD is the strength of my life; of whom shall I be afraid?" (A powerful affirmation of God's protective presence over fear.)
- **Romans 8:15:** "For you did not receive the spirit of bondage again to fear, but you received the Spirit of adoption by whom we cry out, 'Abba, Father.'" (Contrasts the spirit of fear with the Spirit of adoption, which brings intimacy with God.)

Emotional Healing

- **Psalm 147:3:** "He heals the brokenhearted and binds up their wounds." (A comforting promise of God's restorative power for emotional pain.)
- **Jeremiah 30:17:** "For I will restore health to you and heal you of your wounds,' says the LORD." (God's promise of complete restoration, including emotional and physical healing.)
- **2 Corinthians 1:3–4:** "Blessed be the God and Father of our Lord Jesus Christ, the Father of

mercies and God of all comfort, who comforts us in all our tribulation, that we may be able to comfort those who are in any trouble, with the comfort with which we ourselves are comforted by God." (Highlights God's role as the ultimate comforter and the purpose of receiving His comfort.)

Breaking Generational Patterns

- **Exodus 20:5–6:** "You shall not bow down to them nor serve them. For I, the LORD your God, am a jealous God, visiting the iniquity of the fathers upon the children to the third and fourth generations of those who hate Me, but showing mercy to thousands, to those who love Me and keep My commandments." (Explains the concept of generational iniquity and God's mercy.)
- **Galatians 3:13:** "Christ has redeemed us from the curse of the law, having become a curse for us (for it is written, 'Cursed is everyone who hangs on a tree')." (A foundational truth for breaking all curses, including generational ones, through Christ's sacrifice.)
- **Numbers 14:18:** "The LORD is longsuffering and abundant in mercy, forgiving iniquity and transgression; but He by no means clears the guilty, visiting the iniquity of the fathers on the children to the third and fourth generation."

(Reiterates generational consequences but also God's mercy.)

APPENDIX E: COMMON DEMONIC SPIRITS – NAMES & FUNCTIONS

Understanding the common functions of demonic spirits can aid in identifying and addressing them in deliverance. This is not an exhaustive list, but focuses on frequently encountered oppressive spirits.

Name	Function	Reference
Spirit of Infirmity	Causes chronic sickness, weakness, pain, and various physical ailments. Can manifest as undiagnosable conditions or resistance to healing.	Luke 13:11 (Woman bent over for 18 years, whom Jesus called "bound by Satan")
Spirit of Fear	Induces tormenting fear, anxiety, panic attacks, phobias, dread, and paranoia. Often leads to irrational thoughts and behaviors.	2 Timothy 1:7 ("For God has not given us a spirit of fear...")
Spirit of Heaviness	Brings depression, despair, hopelessness, despondency, lethargy, and a sense of being	Isaiah 61:3 ("To give them beauty for ashes, the oil of joy for mourning, the

Name	Function	Reference
	burdened. Can lead to suicidal ideation.	garment of praise for the spirit of heaviness...")
Lying Spirit	Promotes deception, false prophecy, manipulation, self-deception, and an inability to perceive truth. Can operate in religious contexts.	1 Kings 22:22-23 (A lying spirit sent to deceive Ahab's prophets)
Familiar Spirit	Operates through mediums, psychics, and necromancy. Provides false guidance, "revelation" from deceased persons, and occult knowledge. Mimics the Holy Spirit or angels of light.	Leviticus 19:31 ("Do not turn to mediums or consult familiar spirits, for you will be defiled by them...")
Spirit of Divination	Empowers fortune-telling, clairvoyance, psychic abilities, astrology, and other forms of occult foresight. Often connected to financial gain.	Acts 16:16-18 (The slave girl with a spirit of divination)
Spirit of Lust	Fuels sexual immorality, perversion, pornography addiction, adultery, fornication,	Matthew 5:28 (Implied, as lust is a spiritual issue that can

Name	Function	Reference
	and obsessive sexual thoughts. Can manifest as sexual brokenness or identity confusion.	lead to sin. Other passages like 1 John 2:16 discuss the lust of the flesh.)
Spirit of Rebellion	Incites pride, stubbornness, disobedience to authority (God-given and human), defiance, and a refusal to submit. Often leads to a spirit of independence.	1 Samuel 15:23 ("For rebellion is as the sin of witchcraft, and stubbornness is as iniquity and idolatry...")
Spirit of Bondage	Causes a sense of being trapped, enslaved, or unable to break free from sinful habits or patterns. Can lead to self-condemnation.	Romans 8:15 ("For you did not receive the spirit of bondage again to fear...")
Spirit of Poverty	Creates cycles of financial lack, debt, struggle, and limitation. Can be linked to generational curses or ungodly mindsets about money.	Deuteronomy 28 (Contrasts blessings and curses, including financial)
Spirit of Rejection	Instills feelings of being unwanted, unloved, abandoned, unworthy, and	Psalm 27:10 ("When my father and my mother forsake

Name	Function	Reference
	insecure. Can lead to self-hatred, isolation, and difficulty forming healthy relationships.	me, then the LORD will take care of me.") (Implies rejection as a human experience that God redeems)
Spirit of Control	Drives manipulative behaviors, dominance over others, micromanagement, and an inability to trust. Can operate in abusive relationships or religious settings.	3 John 1:9 (Diotrephes, who loved to have preeminence)

APPENDIX F: POST-DELIVERANCE DAILY DECLARATIONS (30 DAYS)

These declarations are crucial for maintaining your freedom after deliverance. Speak them aloud daily, allowing them to renew your mind and fortify your spirit. Consider writing them out and placing them in visible locations.

- **Day 1:** "I am delivered from the power of darkness and translated into the Kingdom of Christ." (Colossians 1:13) - *Affirm your new spiritual address and allegiance.*
- **Day 2:** "The Lord is my strength and my song; He has become my salvation." (Psalm 118:14) - *Declare God as your source of strength and ultimate rescuer.*
- **Day 3:** "I have the mind of Christ." (1 Corinthians 2:16) - *Embrace your spiritual intelligence and ability to think like Jesus.*
- **Day 4:** "I am crucified with Christ; it is no longer I who live, but Christ lives in me; and the life which I now live in the flesh I live by faith in the Son of God, who loved me and gave Himself for me." (Galatians 2:20) - *Embrace your new identity in Christ's death and resurrection.*

- **Day 5:** "I am a temple of the Holy Spirit, and I glorify God in my body and in my spirit, which are God's." (1 Corinthians 6:19-20) - *Affirm your body as God's dwelling place.*
- **Day 6:** "I am more than a conqueror through Him who loved me." (Romans 8:37) - *Declare your victory and triumph in Christ.*
- **Day 7:** "I can do all things through Christ who strengthens me." (Philippians 4:13) - *Reaffirm your capability and empowerment through Jesus.*
- **Day 8:** "The Lord is my Shepherd; I shall not want." (Psalm 23:1) - *Trust in God's provision and guidance.*
- **Day 9:** "I am blessed with all spiritual blessings in heavenly places in Christ." (Ephesians 1:3) - *Claim your spiritual inheritance in Christ.*
- **Day 10:** "The joy of the Lord is my strength." (Nehemiah 8:10) - *Choose joy as your source of resilience.*
- **Day 11:** "I am complete in Him who is the head of all principality and power." (Colossians 2:10) - *Declare your wholeness and sufficiency in Christ.*
- **Day 12:** "I am righteous in Christ Jesus." (2 Corinthians 5:21) - *Embrace your standing of righteousness before God.*
- **Day 13:** "I walk by faith, not by sight." (2 Corinthians 5:7) - *Commit to living by spiritual truth, not circumstances.*

- **Day 14:** "I am rooted and grounded in love." (Ephesians 3:17) - *Declare love as the foundation of your being.*
- **Day 15:** "I am a child of God." (John 1:12) - *Affirm your divine adoption and beloved status.*
- **Day 16:** "God is able to do exceedingly abundantly above all that I ask or think." (Ephesians 3:20) - *Declare God's limitless power in your life.*
- **Day 17:** "I overcome by the blood of the Lamb and the word of my testimony." (Revelation 12:11) - *Affirm your victory through Christ's sacrifice and your declaration.*
- **Day 18:** "I cast all my care upon Him, for He cares for me." (1 Peter 5:7) - *Release burdens and trust in God's care.*
- **Day 19:** "I am forgiven of all my sins, past, present, and future." (Colossians 1:14) - *Rest in the complete forgiveness found in Christ.*
- **Day 20:** "God has not given me a spirit of fear, but of power and of love and of a sound mind." (2 Timothy 1:7) - *Reaffirm your God-given spiritual attributes over fear.*
- **Day 21:** "I am an heir of God and a joint heir with Christ." (Romans 8:17) - *Claim your rich inheritance in God.*
- **Day 22:** "I am redeemed from the curse of the law." (Galatians 3:13) - *Declare freedom from any curses or negative generational patterns.*

- **Day 23:** "I put on the whole armor of God daily." (Ephesians 6:11) - *Commit to spiritual protection and readiness.*
- **Day 24:** "The Lord is my helper; I will not fear what man can do to me." (Hebrews 13:6) - *Trust in divine assistance and overcome fear of man.*
- **Day 25:** "I am light in the Lord." (Ephesians 5:8) - *Live as a reflection of God's light.*
- **Day 26:** "I have the peace of God, which surpasses all understanding." (Philippians 4:7) - *Embrace and protect your inner peace.*
- **Day 27:** "I am established in righteousness; I am far from oppression." (Isaiah 54:14) - *Declare stability and freedom from oppression through righteousness.*
- **Day 28:** "I walk in love, as Christ also has loved us." (Ephesians 5:2) - *Commit to living a life characterized by love.*
- **Day 29:** "I am victorious through Jesus Christ my Lord." (1 Corinthians 15:57) - *Declare ongoing victory in every area.*
- **Day 30:** "I am strong in the Lord and in the power of His might." (Ephesians 6:10) - *End by affirming your strength found in God's power.*

APPENDIX G: DELIVERANCE MINISTRY SESSION

TEMPLATE & INTERVIEW INTAKE FORM

Purpose: To provide a comprehensive, structured, and spiritually sensitive framework for ministers or teams conducting deliverance sessions. This ensures clarity, wise pastoral care, and effective ministry while honoring the individual's journey.

1. Pre-Ministry Instructions for the Individual:

These instructions are vital to prepare the individual's heart and mind for the deliverance session, maximizing openness to the Holy Spirit's work.

- **Spend dedicated time in prayer and worship the night before and the morning of the session.** This helps to quiet the soul, invite the presence of God, and establish a spiritual atmosphere conducive to breakthrough. Focus on acknowledging God's sovereignty and His desire for your freedom.
- **Fast (if physically able) for a half or full day leading up to the session.** Fasting helps to humble oneself before God, sharpen spiritual

sensitivity, and demonstrate a serious commitment to seeking deliverance. If health conditions prevent fasting, encourage alternative forms of spiritual discipline, such as abstaining from certain media or activities.

- **Complete the intake form prayerfully and honestly.** Encourage the individual to be transparent and open, as this information is crucial for the ministry team to understand the areas needing prayer and intervention. Reassure them of confidentiality.

- **Repent of any known sin beforehand.** Encourage a thorough self-examination and sincere repentance for any unconfessed sins. This clears spiritual blockages and aligns the individual's will with God's.

- **Bring any occult items (books, jewelry, amulets, tattoos that can be physically covered/removed, etc.) that need to be destroyed.** These items can serve as legal grounds for demonic attachment and must be renounced and destroyed according to biblical principles (e.g., Acts 19:19). Provide clear instructions on how these items will be handled (e.g., burned, broken).

2. Interview Intake Form (To Be Completed

Before Ministry Session):

This form gathers essential information to help the ministry team tailor the session effectively and provide appropriate spiritual care. **All information should be kept strictly confidential.**

Personal Information:

- Full Name:
- Age:
- Phone/Email:
- Date of Session:
- Emergency Contact (Name & Relationship):

Spiritual Background:

- Are you born again (saved)? ___ Yes ___ No ___ Unsure (If unsure, the team may need to lead them in a salvation prayer first.)
- Have you been water baptized? ___ Yes ___ No
- Have you been baptized in the Holy Spirit (with evidence of speaking in tongues)? ___ Yes ___ No ___ Not Sure
- Do you regularly attend a church? ___ Yes ___ No (If no, discuss importance of consistent fellowship for sustained freedom.)
- Do you have a personal relationship with Jesus Christ? Please describe it briefly.
- What is your understanding of deliverance ministry?

Areas of Concern (Check All That Apply and add specific examples/details if comfortable):

- ___ Fear / Anxiety / Panic Attacks (e.g., social anxiety, phobias, constant worry)
- ___ Depression / Heaviness / Hopelessness (e.g., suicidal thoughts, chronic sadness, apathy)
- ___ Nightmares / Night Terrors / Sleep Paralysis (Describe frequency and content)
- ___ Addictions (Drugs, Alcohol, Pornography, Gambling, Self-harm, Food, Tobacco, etc.) - Please specify:
- ___ Rejection / Abandonment / Self-hatred / Low Self-esteem / Insecurity
- ___ Physical Illness (unexplained or chronic, resisting medical treatment) - Please specify:
- ___ Suicidal Thoughts / Self-harm (History of attempts or urges?)
- ___ Sexual Immorality / Perversion / Trauma (e.g., sexual abuse, promiscuity, same-sex attraction, gender identity confusion, masturbation addiction)
- ___ Witchcraft / Occult / New Age / False Religion (e.g., horoscopes, tarot cards, ouija boards, crystals, yoga as spiritual practice, reiki, ancestral worship, cults) - Please specify involvement:

- ____ Involvement with Psychics, Mediums, Tarot, Fortune Tellers, Astrologers, etc. - Please specify:
- ____ Abuse (verbal, emotional, physical, sexual) - Please describe context:
- ____ Anger / Rage / Uncontrolled Temper
- ____ Bitterness / Unforgiveness / Resentment
- ____ Control / Manipulation / Domination
- ____ Spiritual apathy / Resistance to prayer/Bible reading
- ____ Hearing voices / Seeing things (outside of a diagnosed medical condition)
- ____ Other persistent struggles not listed:

Generational Patterns (Check if Present in Family History for 3-4 generations if known):

- ____ Mental Illness (e.g., schizophrenia, bipolar disorder, severe depression)
- ____ Addiction (Alcohol, Drugs, etc.)
- ____ Divorce / Adultery / Illegitimacy
- ____ Occult / Freemasonry / Secret Societies / Cults (Specify if known)
- ____ Poverty / Constant Lack / Financial curses
- ____ Premature Death / Suicide / Accidents
- ____ Chronic Illness / Specific diseases (e.g., cancer, diabetes)
- ____ Abuse (physical, sexual, emotional)
- ____ Unexplained misfortunes or repeated failures

Soul Ties or Ungodly Relationships to Renounce (List names of individuals or types of relationships that need to be severed due to ungodly connection):

- (e.g., former sexual partners, abusive relationships, manipulative friendships, ungodly mentors)

Known Traumas or Entry Points (Accidents, Abuse, Betrayal, Shock, Deep Wounds, etc. - briefly describe impact):

- (e.g., car accident leading to chronic fear, childhood abuse leading to rejection, betrayal leading to bitterness)

Desired Outcome from Session:

- What do you hope to receive from this deliverance session?

3. Deliverance Ministry Session Structure:

This structure provides a clear flow for the session, ensuring all critical aspects of deliverance and aftercare are addressed.

I. Welcome and Worship (10–15 minutes)

- **Warm Welcome & Prayer:** Begin with a genuine welcome, put the individual at ease, and open with a prayer acknowledging God's presence and inviting the Holy Spirit to lead the session.

- **Brief Scripture Reading:** Choose a relevant Scripture emphasizing God's love, power, and desire for freedom (e.g., John 8:36, Isaiah 61:1).
- **Invite the Holy Spirit:** Explicitly state the desire for the Holy Spirit to take full control and illuminate every hidden area. Play gentle worship music if appropriate to create a reverent atmosphere.

II. Review of Intake Form (5–10 minutes)

- **Discussion and Clarification:** Go through the intake form with the individual. Ask open-ended questions to clarify details, gain deeper understanding, and identify any additional areas of concern.
- **Ensure Readiness and Willingness:** Confirm that the person is truly ready and willing to receive freedom, commit to repentance, and maintain their deliverance. Address any hesitations or misunderstandings about the process.
- **Emphasize God's Love:** Reassure them that the goal is not to shame but to bring healing and freedom through God's love and power.

III. Repentance & Renunciation (15–20 minutes)

- **Lead in Specific Repentance:** Guide the individual in heartfelt repentance for *their own sins* (e.g., unforgiveness, pride, fear, involvement in occult, sexual sin). Be specific as revealed by the intake form or Holy Spirit.
- **Lead in Renunciation of Ungodly Soul Ties:** Specifically address and break ungodly soul ties as identified on the form. Guide them to verbally renounce the connection and any associated spirits.
- **Lead in Renunciation of Covenants, Curses, and Occult Practices:** Guide the individual to verbally renounce all involvement with occult practices, false religions, specific curses (including generational curses), and any ungodly vows or dedications. **It is crucial for the individual to speak these renunciations aloud.**
- **Breaking Legal Grounds:** Explain that through repentance and renunciation, they are closing the doors and breaking the legal grounds that the enemy has used.

IV. Deliverance Prayer (20–45 minutes)

- **Pray in the Name of Jesus:** Begin praying with authority, declaring freedom in the name of Jesus Christ.
- **Command Spirits to Leave:** Address spirits by name and function as revealed through the intake form, discernment, or spiritual manifestations

(e.g., "Spirit of Fear, I command you to leave now in the name of Jesus!"). Be bold and direct.

- **Laying on Hands & Anointing Oil:** Lay hands on the individual (only with express permission, usually on the shoulders or head) as a point of contact for prayer. Anointing oil can be used symbolically if desired, signifying consecration and the anointing of the Holy Spirit.

- **Address Manifestations:** Remain calm and authoritative if manifestations occur (e.g., coughing, yawning, crying, physical discomfort). Do not be distracted or intimidated. Instruct the individual to cooperate by expelling (coughing, spitting) as needed.

- **Focus on Release:** Continue praying until a sense of release, peace, or lightness is clearly experienced by the individual and discerned by the team.

- **Pray for Inner Healing (Concurrent or Sequential):** As spirits are cast out, pray for the healing of the underlying emotional wounds or trauma that provided entry points for those spirits. This is often interwoven with the deliverance prayer.

V. Infilling & Restoration (10–15 minutes)

- **Invite the Holy Spirit to Fill:** Once spirits are expelled, immediately invite the Holy Spirit to fill every cleansed area with His presence, peace, love, and righteousness. This prevents spirits from returning (Matthew 12:43-45).

- **Pray for Emotional Healing, Identity, and Peace:** Specifically pray for the healing of any remaining emotional pain, for a strong sense of their true identity in Christ, and for the peace of God to flood their heart and mind.
- **Declare Prophetic Words of Restoration and Destiny:** Speak affirming, life-giving, and Scripture-based declarations over the individual, affirming their freedom, purpose, and future in Christ.

VI. Post-Ministry Debrief & Instructions

- **Encouragement and Affirmation:** Affirm the work God has done and encourage the individual in their new freedom.
- **Instruction on Maintaining Freedom:**
  - **Daily Devotion:** Emphasize the importance of daily reading the Word of God, prayer, and worship to build spiritual strength.
  - **Accountability:** Encourage seeking out a trusted Christian mentor or small group for ongoing support and accountability.
  - **Filling the Vacuum:** Explain the importance of "filling the vacuum" with God's presence and truth, so expelled spirits do not return.

- o **Spiritual Warfare:** Teach them about standing firm against temptation and how to resist the enemy.
- o **Water Baptism:** If not yet water baptized, encourage them to do so as a public declaration of their faith and new life.
- **Provide Resources:** Hand out daily declaration sheets (like Appendix F), relevant Scripture lists, and contact information for follow-up.
- **Suggest Follow-up or Counseling:** If deeper issues or long-term struggles remain (e.g., severe trauma, addiction, relationship issues), suggest professional Christian counseling or ongoing discipleship.

Sample Follow-up Questions (to be asked immediately after the session and potentially in subsequent days/weeks):

- Do you feel lighter, clearer, more peaceful, or have you experienced a significant shift in your spirit or emotions?
- Was there any particular moment of release, breakthrough, or a specific spirit you felt leave?
- Did you have any dreams, visions, or sensations during the session that should be noted?
- How do you feel about your identity in Christ now?

- What is your next step in maintaining this freedom?

Important Notes for Ministers:

- **Always minister in teams of two or more.** This provides accountability, discernment, support, and ensures a witness.
- **Keep confidential records securely.** Maintain detailed but discreet notes for pastoral care and follow-up.
- **Never force or coerce manifestations.** Allow the Holy Spirit to work naturally. Focus on commanding spirits in Jesus' name, not on forcing physical reactions.
- **Be gentle, bold, and Spirit-led.** Combine compassion and care with unwavering authority in Christ. Discernment is key to knowing when to be gentle and when to be firm.
- **Prioritize the individual's safety and well-being.** If there are concerns about mental health, ensure proper referral to qualified professionals is made. Deliverance ministry complements, but does not replace, professional medical or psychological care.
- **Maintain a posture of humility and reliance on the Holy Spirit.** Remember that it is Christ who delivers, not human effort.

APPENDIX H: GLOSSARY OF DELIVERANCE TERMS

Understanding these terms provides a common language for discussing and engaging in deliverance ministry.

Anointing

The supernatural empowerment of the Holy Spirit that enables believers to minister with divine authority. In deliverance, the anointing breaks spiritual yokes (Isaiah 10:27), rendering demonic oppression powerless.

Binding and Loosing

Based on Matthew 18:18. Binding refers to restricting demonic activity; loosing refers to releasing God's power, healing, or angelic assistance. Both are strategic in spiritual warfare and deliverance.

Bloodline Curse / Generational Curse

Demonic patterns, behaviors, or afflictions passed through family lineage due to iniquities, occult involvement, or unrepented sin. These must be broken through confession, repentance, and the application of the blood of Jesus (Exodus 20:5).

Breakthrough

A moment of spiritual freedom when strongholds, bondages, or hindrances are broken, allowing for healing, clarity, and victory. Often follows repentance, prayer, or deliverance.

Casting Out (Ekballō – ἐκβάλλω)

The forceful expelling of a demon from an individual by the authority of Jesus Christ (Mark 16:17). It is not a negotiation, but a command issued under divine authority.

Daimonizomai

(Greek: δαιμονίζομαι) A New Testament term meaning "to be afflicted by a demon" or "under demonic influence." It does not necessarily imply total possession, but rather includes varying degrees of torment, oppression, or demonic activity affecting a person's body, mind, or emotions.

Deliverance

The process, through the authority of Jesus Christ and the power of the Holy Spirit, of identifying, confronting, and casting out evil spirits. Deliverance also includes inner healing and renewing the mind to help maintain spiritual freedom.

Entry Points (Gateways or Doors)

Access points through which demons gain legal or spiritual access to a person's life. Common entry points include sexual sin, trauma, witchcraft, generational sin, unforgiveness, and unhealed emotional wounds.

Familiar Spirits

Demons that impersonate deceased loved ones, ancestors, or personal spirits to deceive individuals. Often operate through mediums, psychics, or occult rituals. Forbidden by Scripture (Leviticus 19:31).

Inner Healing

The Spirit-led process of healing past emotional wounds, trauma, and rejection. Inner healing is essential in deliverance, as unhealed wounds may serve as legal ground for demonic oppression or strongholds.

Jezebel Spirit

A high-level controlling, manipulative, and seductive spirit. It often works through wounded individuals and seeks to usurp authority, dominate leadership, or corrupt spiritual discernment. Referenced in Revelation 2:20.

Legal Ground

Any unresolved sin, wound, agreement, or covenant that gives demons permission to operate. This includes unconfessed sin, inner vows, unforgiveness, occult activity, and trauma. Deliverance involves closing legal ground through repentance and renunciation.

Manifestation

A visible or audible response (shaking, screaming, vomiting, contortions, etc.) indicating a demon's presence or resistance during deliverance. Not to be feared, but recognized as part of spiritual expulsion.

Marine Spirits

A class of demonic entities often linked to water-based mythology and sexual sin. Common in global deliverance contexts (e.g., Leviathan, spirit spouses). These spirits influence identity, seduction, and emotional manipulation.

Open Doors

Spiritual vulnerabilities—often through sin, trauma, or ignorance—that grant demons access. Deliverance involves identifying and closing these doors with the Word and the power of the Holy Spirit.

Oppression

Demonic influence that harasses, torments, or hinders a person's life without full possession. It affects the mind, emotions, and body, manifesting through fear, depression, addiction, or chronic illness.

Principalities and Powers

High-ranking demonic rulers in Satan's kingdom. Referenced in Ephesians 6:12, they influence nations, systems, and regions. These are confronted through strategic intercession and apostolic authority.

Renunciation

A vocal, willful rejection of sin, demonic pacts, curses, or ungodly agreements. Renunciation severs ties with darkness and aligns the believer with the authority of Christ.

Soul Tie

A deep emotional, psychological, or spiritual bond between two individuals. Godly soul ties strengthen healthy relationships (e.g., marriage), while ungodly soul ties—formed through fornication, manipulation, or control—can serve as demonic pathways.

Stronghold

A fortified mental or emotional structure built on lies, trauma, or sin. It resists the truth of God's Word and must be dismantled by renewing the mind (2 Corinthians 10:4–5). Examples include fear, pride, addiction, or rejection.

Territorial Spirit

A demon assigned to govern a specific region, institution, family line, or people group. These spirits require persistent, strategic spiritual warfare to dislodge.

Transfer of Spirits

The transference of demonic influence from one person to another, often through laying on of hands, sexual contact, or close relational proximity. Proper spiritual covering and discernment are essential to prevent transfers.

Trespasser Spirit

A demon illegally operating in the life of a believer. While it has no legal right under the blood of Jesus, it may remain due to unclosed doors or ignorance. Deliverance removes the trespasser and restores spiritual order.

Unforgiveness

A major legal ground for demonic access. Holding onto bitterness or resentment opens the soul to tormentors (Matthew 18:34–35). Forgiveness is essential to freedom.

Word of Knowledge

A revelatory gift of the Holy Spirit used to reveal hidden information, such as the source of bondage, the name of a spirit, or a root issue in deliverance ministry (1 Corinthians 12:8).

Yoke

A spiritual burden or bondage imposed through sin or demonic oppression. The anointing breaks the yoke and brings liberty (Isaiah 10:27).

BIBLIOGRAPHY

Anderson, Neil T. *The Bondage Breaker*. Eugene, OR: Harvest House Publishers, 1990. Revised edition, 1993.

Arnold, Eberhard. *The Early Christians: In Their Own Words*. Farmington, PA: Plough Publishing House, 2007.

Brown, Rebecca. *He Came to Set the Captives Free*. New Kensington, PA: Whitaker House, 1986.

Brown, Rebecca. *Prepare for War*. New Kensington, PA: Whitaker House, 1987.

Goll, James W. *Deliverance from Darkness: A Study Guide*. Shippensburg, PA: Destiny Image, 2011.

Goll, James W. *The Seer: The Prophetic Power of Visions, Dreams, and Open Heavens*. Shippensburg, PA: Destiny Image, 2004.

Hammond, Frank, and Ida Mae Hammond. *Pigs in the Parlor: A Practical Guide to Deliverance*. Kirkwood, MO: Impact Christian Books, 1973. Revised edition, 2008.

Heiser, Michael S. *The Unseen Realm: Recovering the Supernatural Worldview of the Bible*. Bellingham, WA: Lexham Press, 2015.

Kylstra, Chester, and Betsy Kylstra. *Biblical Healing and Deliverance: A Guide to Experiencing Freedom from Sins of the Past, Destructive Beliefs, Emotional and Spiritual Pain, Curses and Oppression*. Grand Rapids, MI: Chosen Books, 2005.

Lucero, Linda Rios. *Lucifer's War: The Battle for Your Soul*. Lake Mary, FL: Creation House, 2004.

Prince, Derek. *They Shall Expel Demons: What You Need to Know about Demons—Your Invisible Enemies*. Grand Rapids, MI: Chosen Books, 1998.

Reese, Andy. *Freedom Tools for Overcoming Life's Tough Problems: A Guide for Broken Hearts and Wounded Lives*. Grand Rapids, MI: Chosen Books, 2008.

Sandford, John Loren, and Mark Sandford. *Deliverance and Inner Healing*. Grand Rapids, MI: Chosen Books, 1992. Revised edition, 2008.

Smalley, Gary, and John Trent. *The Blessing: Giving the Gift of Unconditional Love and Acceptance*. Nashville, TN: Thomas Nelson, 2004..

About the Author

Dr. Damian A. Hinton, Sr., MDiv, MTh, DMin, is a seasoned apostolic leader, pastor, author, and global teacher committed to seeing lives transformed by the power of God's Word and the ministry of the Holy Spirit. With over three decades of ministry experience, he is the founding and senior pastor of **Life Changing Ministries**, based in Maryland, and the visionary behind **The Apostolic Network of International Churches and Ministries (ANICM)**.

Dr. Hinton's passion for deliverance, healing, and inner restoration flows from both a deep biblical foundation and personal experience. Having witnessed firsthand the power of God to set captives free, he equips the Body of Christ to walk in victory through sound doctrine, prophetic insight, and practical application. His ministry has impacted nations, training leaders, establishing churches, and raising up ministers who walk in kingdom authority.

He holds degrees in Philosophy from Morgan State University and graduate theological degrees from Liberty University, including a Doctor of Ministry. Dr. Hinton is also a devoted husband to **Overseer Cheryl Hinton**, and together they are spiritual parents, mentors, and shepherds to many. They have five children and several grandchildren, forming a legacy of faith and generational impact.

As a prolific writer, Dr. Hinton has authored works on leadership, spiritual growth, theology, and personal transformation. Through his preaching, teaching, and writing, he remains committed to helping others embrace their identity in Christ, break free from spiritual bondage, and walk in wholeness and purpose.

Made in the USA
Middletown, DE
15 November 2025

20601984R00189